LIFE-CHANGING
LEADERSHIP HABITS

LIFE-CHANGING LEADERSHIP HABITS

10 Proven Principles
That Will Elevate People, Profit, and Purpose

DR JEFF DOOLITTLE

Copyrighted Material

Life-Changing Leadership Habits:
10 Proven Principles That Will Elevate People, Profit, and Purpose

Copyright © 2023 by Dr. Jeff Doolittle. All Rights Reserved.

No part of this publication may be reproduced, stored in a retrieval system or transmitted, in any form or by any means—electronic, mechanical, photocopying, recording or otherwise—without prior written permission from the publisher, except for the inclusion of brief quotations in a review.

For information about this title or to order other books and/or electronic media, for keynote and workshops, for executive coaching, for organizational consulting, contact the publisher:

Organizational Talent Consulting
info@organizationaltalent.com
www.lifechangingleadershiphabits.com
www.organizationaltalent.com

ISBNs:
979-8-9871919-2-7 (hardcover)
979-8-9871919-0-3 (softcover)
979-8-9871919-1-0 (eBook)

Printed in the United States of America

Cover and Interior design: 1106 Design

Although the publisher and the author have made every effort to ensure that the information in this book was correct at press time and while this publication is designed to provide accurate information in regard to the subject matter covered, the publisher and the author assume no responsibility for errors, inaccuracies, omissions, or any other inconsistencies herein and hereby disclaim any liability to any party for any loss, damage, or disruption caused by errors or omissions, whether such errors or omissions result from negligence, accident, or any other cause.

Unless otherwise indicated, all the names, characters, businesses, places, events and incidents in the fables included in this book are either the product of the author's imagination or used in a fictitious manner. Any resemblance to actual persons, living or dead, or actual events is purely coincidental.

*This book is dedicated to Kelly,
the love of my life.*

life-chang·ing

An extremely big effect strong enough to change the life of someone and the world.

lead·er·ship

To turn vision into reality; selfless influence of worthy performance; to bring out the best in followers.

hab·its

Routines, patterns, or practices performed regularly; automatic responses to a specific situation.

Contents

Introduction   **xi**
    Who Really Needs to Read and Use This Guide?   xi
    Why This Book Will Benefit You   xii
    How to Use This Everyday Guide   xiv

Part One: The Fundamentals   **1**
    Being the Leader the Contemporary World Needs   3
    The Inner and Outer Game   5
    The Role of Virtues, Character, and Values   7
    The Role of Traits   11
    The Role of Others   13
    The Role of Culture   17
    What Are Worldview Forces and Why Are They Important?   21
    Why Effective Leadership Makes the Difference   23
    What Are the 10 Worst Leadership Habits?   27
    Two Important Questions   31

Part Two: 10 Life-Changing Habits   **33**
    Life-Changing Habit #1: Loving Followers   35
    Life-Changing Habit #2: Focusing on Strengths   55

Life-Changing Habit #3: Embracing Data-Driven Decisions	71
Life-Changing Habit #4: Maximizing Purpose	89
Life-Changing Habit #5: Living in Balance	113
Life-Changing Habit #6: Excelling in Management	135
Life-Changing Habit #7: Mastering Difficult Conversations	155
Life-Changing Habit #8: Being Trustworthy	179
Life-Changing Habit #9: Embracing Failure	195
Life-Changing Habit #10: Thinking Strategically	211

Part Three: Secrets to Leading with Life-Changing Habits — **227**

Answering Questions and Anticipating Problems	229
Are There Any Downsides to Building Life-Changing Habits?	239
Concluding Thoughts	243

Appendix — **245**

What Should You Read Next?	247
Bonus Resources	249
Acknowledgments	251
Accidental Habit Assessment	253
Index	255
About the Author	265
Organizational Talent Consulting Solutions	267

Introduction

> "We are what we repeatedly do. Excellence,
> then, is not an act, but a habit."
> —WILL DURANT[1]

> "Probably more has been written and less is known about
> leadership than any other topic in the behavioral sciences."
> —WARREN G. BENNIS[2]

Who Really Needs to Read and Use This Guide?

There are at least three categories of leaders who need to be aware of and practice the advice this guide provides: (1) successful executives and business owners who are seeking ways to get more out of life and work; (2) executives and business owners whose careers are stalling or who feel they are not living their best life, and need a practical plan to give their career a boost; and (3) high-potential leaders who aspire to maximize the impact of their careers and get the most out of life and work.

This everyday guide is intentionally short, to the point, and organized as a reference tool. I recognize that leaders are running on a metaphorical treadmill at work. Time is precious and a limited resource. The topic of effective leadership does not need to be complicated and time-consuming. Some of the simplest solutions to life's most significant problems can have the greatest impact on your life.

Why This Book Will Benefit You

Leaders must continually develop and evolve at a pace consistent with the change in our exacting world. Entropy is a fundamental concept governing life and work. Entropy is defined as disorder and randomness in a natural system; the second law in thermodynamics states that left unchecked, entropy increases with time in closed systems. Leaders with closed minds and organizations closed to new ideas quickly fall behind and become obsolete.

The bad habits of leadership that we have all witnessed or engaged in are not destiny. One of the greatest myths I encounter in coaching leaders and business owners is that they believe their current reality reflects a permanent reality. We don't stay the same. Even passions and proficiency can change. In my life, I have experienced firsthand and learned from thought leaders in the field of strategic leadership how to apply proven solutions to create life-changing habits. I believe you would like to do so as well.

Business executives naturally desire to get more out of life and work. But privately, they question if it is possible, given the expectations from their board members, shareholders, and key stakeholders. In today's business environment, success and significance appear to be competing priorities and opposite ends on a vice-and-virtue continuum. In the following pages, I share ways to bend the continuum line of thinking where it is "either this or that" and consider holistic solutions of "both this and that" thinking.

Striving for life-changing habits is a competitive advantage available to any leader looking for a powerful point of differentiation. This book draws on the latest research within the workplace, so leaders don't waste their time on solutions that sound good but fail to achieve lasting

INTRODUCTION

results. These ideas are grounded in the fields of psychology, philosophy, biology, and neuroscience. My contribution is to synthesize the best ideas and new connections of ideas into highly practical ways for leading with life-changing habits and breaking ten of the worst leadership habits that derail leaders.

While work and the workplace are continually changing, the life-changing habits and proven solutions identified in this book are timeless. Leaders can rely on the lasting principles year-over-year to grow personally and professionally. You can use these principles to build a career, a business, and a life.

Of course, there is no single best approach to effective leadership. However, the ideas on the pages that follow challenge the notion presented by H. L. Mencken that "There is always a well-known solution to every human problem—neat, plausible, and wrong."[3] These ten life-changing habits are clear, simple, and proven to create lasting results.

Research constantly reminds us that the best and most creative leaders populate the most successful organizations. I sincerely hope this book is helpful to you, your team, your organization, and our world.

All the best!
Dr. Jeff Doolittle

Endnotes

1. Durant, W. (1991). *The Story of Philosophy: The Lives and Opinions of the Greater Philosophers.* (2nd ed.) Pocket Books.
2. Bennis, W. G. (1959). "Leadership Theory and Administrative Behavior: The Problem of Authority." *Administrative Science Quarterly,* 4(3), 259-301.
3. Mencken. H. L. (2016). *Prejudices: Second Series.* Project Gutenberg.

How to Use This Everyday Guide

Most people pick up a guide and begin by thumbing through the chapters and looking at the various tables and illustrations. This book is designed to help leaders lead with life-changing habits and focus on the pressing, readily visible ways in which a bad habit can show up for them. This book provides illustrations of leadership habits across a vice-virtue continuum to aid recognition.

Simply stated, a vice does not lead to happiness, and a virtue leads to a positive outcome in life and work. Leadership is best recognized along an often-paradoxical continuum between right and right, rather than just either/or choices that leaders make.

A glance through this book reveals that it is organized around three distinct parts. Part One, titled The Fundamentals, provides a call to action for being the leader the contemporary world needs, the inner and outer game at play in every situation, the foundational roles (virtues, character, traits, others, and culture), why effective leadership makes the difference, a quick overview of the ten worst leadership habits, and two critical questions you need to consider before getting started.

Part Two is organized around the ten life-changing habits. Each chapter in this section includes a concise overview of a life-changing habit, associated virtues, a short story or fable taken from the workplace, examples to help identify related vices, and a discussion of the causes, consequences, and complications associated with each bad habit. Each chapter in Part Two concludes with key chapter summary points and a few reflective questions to expand your thinking on leading with each life-changing habit.

Part Three, the final part of the book, shifts the attention onto the secrets to life-changing habits. This section wrestles with common questions and obstacles for leading with life-changing habits, the potential downsides of breaking bad leadership habits, and concludes with a personal challenge.

INTRODUCTION

Some of you will enjoy reading this guide from cover-to-cover and using the reflection questions and transformational tools as you go. However, I have a few shortcuts to offer, in case you don't have the time to work through the entire book right now.

- **If you are not aware of your leadership habits:** Turn to this guide's Appendix and use the link provided to complete the Accidental Habit Assessment. In addition to increasing awareness, the free report you receive can serve as a personalized reading guide to help you get the most value out of this book in the least amount of time.
- **If you have only five to ten minutes to read:** After finding the specific chapter to read from the table of contents, turn to the chapter's summary key points at the end, then skim the overview and transformational tools sections.
- **If you have twenty minutes and a good idea of where you need to focus:** Read the quick overview of the ten worst leadership habits in Part One, then use the table of contents to navigate to the life-changing habit chapter you need.

The reflection questions and transformational tools at the end of each chapter in Part Two will help you continue your leadership development journey. Additionally, you won't want to miss out on the bonus resources found in the Appendix for added value.

• • •

PART ONE

The Fundamentals

"Get the fundamentals down, and the level of everything you do will rise."
—MICHAEL JORDAN[1]

Endnotes

1. Jordan, M. (1994). *I Can't Accept Not Trying: Michael Jordan on the Pursuit of Excellence.* HarperCollins Publishers.

Being the Leader the Contemporary World Needs

Sadly, the silence of most leaders on today's challenges of corruption, violence, and the environmental disasters facing society is deafening. The World Economic Forum has sounded the alarm on a global leadership crisis. Ethical leadership failures span social, political, religious, and business institutions, and the consequences of these failures are increasingly more common and severe. Fines for compliance violations are at all-time highs and point to a serious global trend. The world is desperately in need of better leadership.

Leader failures amount to leadership failure. Leaders have the potential to be catalysts for change, and the world is looking to leadership to be a light in the darkness. However, there is a widespread failure by leaders to accept responsibility outside of the boardroom and to actively lead when it comes to society's challenges.

Leaders, organizations, and communities are far more connected than is often understood. Minor changes by leaders create ripples within organizations that can lead to waves of changes in the lives of employees, their friends and families, and their communities. Experienced leaders understand the fallacy of the saying *What happens at work stays at work and what happens at home stays at home.*

Trust is a key component of organizational effectiveness and is fundamental to the leader-follower relationship. Edelman, a leading global communications company that tracks and publishes a trust index, found that trust in executive leadership directly impacts employee retention, organizational commitment, and change.[1] A leader's credibility, competence, and ethical behavior are foundational elements of trust in the workplace and are damaged by a lack of transparency and credibility of information shared within organizations.

No organization is looking to stay the same. The status quo is not a competitive business strategy. In a turbulent and fast-paced digital workplace, change is increasingly present and difficult. A failure to change leads to business failure. Values influence change behaviors. Merely addressing leader behavior does not lead to lasting organizational change. Being a leader the contemporary world needs requires that leaders move beyond developing behaviors and begin developing virtues and character. It is not an issue of either behaviors or virtues but of both behaviors and virtues that establish life-changing habits.

• • •

Endnotes
1. Edelman, R. (2020). 2020 Edelman Trust Barometer. Edelman.

The Inner and Outer Game

There are two games at play with each life-changing habit: an inner game and an outer game. The inner game is quietly at work controlling the outer game.[1]

Habits are the observable routines shaped by the inner game. Like a new piece of technology in the workplace, a technology's features or a leader's outer-game behaviors and habits often get the most attention. Still, a technology's operating system or a leader's inner-game traits, virtues, character, and values deserve equal attention and focus. A leader's inner game influences every aspect of their significance and professional success.

Successfully leading with life-changing habits comes from taking an integrative approach to understanding and transforming a leader's inner and outer game.

. . .

Endnotes
1. Anderson, R. & Adams, W. (2016). *Mastering Leadership: An Integrated Framework for Breakthrough Performance and Extraordinary Business Results.* John Wiley & Sons, Inc.

The Role of Virtues, Character, and Values

A leader's virtues, character, and values provide insights for leading with life-changing habits. Aristotle considered virtues a habit or disposition to think, act, or feel in the right way that is not deficient or in excess and toward a good goal.[1] Virtues are a part of an individual's character. Virtues influence personal values. When presented with a new or unknown situation, which accounts for most leadership situations, a leader's virtues and character will govern the actions taken.[2] The following figure is a model that depicts the relationship between virtues, character, and values that drive habits that result in performance outcomes.

Virtues and character are often considered complex and challenging topics to articulate and measure, minimizing their discussion. However, life-changing leadership habits involve a combination of competence, character, and commitment to challenging work. Although not frequently discussed in the workplace, character has been perceived to be foundational to good leadership for many years. Several studies demonstrate the proven benefits associated with virtues and character. One study of

CEOs found that leaders with higher character ratings had a return on net assets of nearly five times of those rated lower.[3] A large-scale empirical study on the influence of virtues on employee and customer identification, distinctiveness, and satisfaction found a significant positive correlation with all dimensions.[4] In another study, researchers surprisingly discovered that virtues had a more substantial positive significance on organizational performance than did organizational management control systems.[5] While leadership habits prescribe what a leader should do in a given situation, a leader's character will decide what a leader will do.

Like competencies, values, character, and virtues can be developed. According to a neo-Aristotelian view of virtue and character development, an individual's development should include knowledge transfer, reasoning, and practice.[6] Character development is primarily developed through role modeling, including feedback and reflection. However, feedback on values, character, and gaps in virtues are not commonly provided, given the complexity of these conversations. Additionally, leaders typically spend little to no time reflecting on character experiences because of ethical blind spots.

Engaging a skillful, dedicated coach can improve character feedback and purposeful character reflection. Dedicated mentors can also support character development by openly reflecting on insights gained from experience.

• • •

Endnotes
1. Pakaluk, M. (2005). *Aristotle's Nicomachean Ethics: An Introduction.* Cambridge University Press. doi:10.1017/CBO9780511802041
2. Badaracco, Jr. (1997). *Defining Moments: When Managers Must Choose Between Right and Right.* Harvard Business School Press.
3. Kiel, F. (2015). *Return on Character: The Real Reason Leaders and Their Companies Win.* Harvard Business Review Press.

4. Chun, R. (2017). "Organizational Virtue and Performance: An Empirical Study of Customers and Employees." *Journal of Business Ethics*, 146(4), 869-881. doi:10.1007/s10551-016-3262-z
5. Donada, C., Mothe, C., Nogatchewsky, G., & de Campos Ribeiro, G. (2019). "The Respective Effects of Virtues and Inter-organizational Management Control Systems on Relationship Quality and Performance: Virtues Win." *Journal of Business Ethics*, 154(1), 211-228.
6. Jubilee Centre for Character and Virtues. (2017). "A Framework for Character Education in Schools." *University of Birmingham*. Online at: www.jubileecentre.ac.uk

The Role of Traits

Are you destined to have certain leadership habits? Do the traits of a leader determine their habits? These questions are important to consider as you seek to understand the role traits play in leading with life-changing habits. Not surprisingly, research has revealed that personality traits have a significant influence on a leader's behavior, especially when the leader has the freedom to make choices.[1]

The most widely accepted trait framework is the Five-Factor Model (FFM), which suggests that openness, conscientiousness, extraversion, agreeableness, and neuroticism are the building blocks of personality. These factors are a causal force on patterns of thought, feelings, and actions.[2] The American Psychology Association describes the five factors as:[3]

- Openness—Open to new experiences from a visual, cultural, or intellectual perspective
- Conscientiousness—Reliable, efficient, responsible, and hardworking
- Extraversion—Talkative, outgoing, sociable, and openly expressive
- Agreeableness—Cooperative and unselfish
- Neuroticism—A lack of emotional predictability and a tendency to struggle with emotions like anxiety

Clear connections between habits[4] and leadership personality[5] traits exist. The good news is that it is possible for leaders to make changes to behavior through persistent interventions. Leaders are not destined to have certain leadership habits.

• • •

Endnotes
1. Judge, T., & Zapata, C. (2015). "The Person-Situation Debate Revisited: Effect of Situation Strength and Trait Activation on the Validity of the Big Five Personality Traits in Predicting Job Performance." *Academy of Management Journal*, 58(4), 1149-1179. https://doi.org/10.5465/amj.2010.0837
2. McCrae, R.R., & John, O.P. (1992). "An Introduction to the Five-Factor Model and Its Applications." *Journal of Personality*, 60(2), 175-215. https://doi.org/10.1111/j.1467-6494.1992.tb00970.x
3. Vandenbos, G.R., ed. American Psychological Association. (n.d.). *APA Dictionary of Psychology*. American Psychological Association. Retrieved January 17, 2022, from https://dictionary.apa.org/
4. Egan, V., & Parmar, R. (2013). "Dirty Habits? Online Pornography Use, Personality, Obsessionality, and Compulsivity." *Journal of Sex & Marital Therapy*, 39(5), 394-409. https://doi.org/10.1080/0092623X.2012.710182
5. Langford, P., Dougall, C., & Parkes, L. (2017). "Measuring leader behaviour: Evidence for a 'big five' model of leadership." *Leadership & Organization Development Journal*, 38(1), 126-144. https://doi.org/10.1108/LODJ-05-2015-0103

The Role of Others

Understanding the influence of others can help you lead with life-changing habits. Social facilitation is a psychological concept relating to the tendency for the influence of others to improve a person's performance on a task. A researcher first described this concept in a study of bicyclists' racing performance in 1898.[1] The researcher noticed that when racing against others, athletes performed better than those racing against their own times. Social facilitation is defined as improvement in performance induced by real, implied, or imagined presence. Social facilitation is thought to impact our drive to perform, our ability to focus while performing, and effectively influence our anxiety and desire to impress others.

Social facilitation has two types of effects:[2]

- **Co-action effects:** referring to performance improvement because others are doing the same task as you
- **Audience effects:** referring to performance improvement because you are doing something in front of others

When considering the role of others on our habits, it is crucial to understand three nuances that impact social facilitation:[3]

- The presence of others negatively influences employee performance on tasks considered complex and challenging.
- The presence of others positively influences employee performance when confidence is high for the task. The presence of others negatively affects employee performance when the performer has lower levels of confidence.
- Proximity, the number of others, and the degree to which others are supportive play a role in influencing performance positively or negatively.

To put this concept into context, one of my first not-so-fun memories associated with the social facilitation audience effect came from an experience I had at eight years old. My parents' desire to develop music appreciation in me led them to make me take one year of piano lessons. I was assigned to play "Doo-Dad Boogie" for my first piano recital. While this sheet music is elementary, it was challenging for a first-year piano student. I was terrified at the recital, despite playing for only a few parents and other students in my piano teacher's living room. This experience reinforced that I played better in private.

Later, in high school, I connected with the positive influence of the social facilitation co-action effect. I was never a great student in grade school. Most of the time, I was a quiet average student. However, when in classes populated with the brightest students, I tended to push myself harder and do better. This elevated performance stood out because I anticipated a major challenge when competing in the higher-level courses.

It might be surprising, but your performance as a leader is not just dependent on you. Isolation is not helpful for you or the organization's bottom line. The following are a couple of tips for applying the social facilitation research to leading with life-changing habits:

- **Practice should be private.** Work toward becoming fluent with a task before performing in front of others. Fluency is the combination of being both accurate and quick. As your fluency increases, task difficulty will decrease. At this point, start to make your performance visible to others to leverage the positive effects of social facilitation. For example, when you become fluent, invite your leader to join in on a virtual project meeting or ask to pair up with someone on an assignment to positively influence your performance.

- **Be thoughtful of those you invite to practice.** Surround yourself with supportive people as you are learning complex tasks. An unsupportive audience harms complex task performance. In an ideal world, everyone would be supportive of your development and practice. They would be sensitive to your needs and ask tactfully about how things are going and about resources. But co-workers and leaders aren't always as supportive as they could or should be.

• • •

Endnotes
1. Aiello, J., & Douthitt, E. (2001). "Social facilitation theory from Triplett to electronic performance monitoring." *Group Dynamics*, 5(3), 163-180.
2. Feinberg, J. & Aiello, J. (2006). Social Facilitation: A Test of Competing Theories. *Journal of Applied Social Psychology*, 36(5), 1087-1109.
3. ibid.,1087-1109.

The Role of Culture

Organizational culture is one of those things that influences everything in a business. It directly impacts organizational success, employees, customers, communities, and leadership habits. The underlying cultural values of an organization affect the behaviors of employees and their decisions. Scholarly research directly linked the effects of an organization's culture on customer satisfaction, employee teamwork, cohesion, employee involvement, and innovation.[1] Just as some organizational culture characteristics can support these qualities, others can inhibit these qualities. For example, a hierarchical corporate culture type is proven to decrease an organization's ability to innovate.[2]

The idea of organizational culture is abstract and often not well understood. The word culture gets used in different ways by people at different times. Culture has been studied for many years, resulting in many models and definitions. Organizational culture is complex because it involves individuals, their interactions, teams, and the organization. Edgar Schein, who is considered one of the most influential contemporary thought leaders on organizational culture, described it as:

"A pattern of shared basic assumptions that the group learned as it solved its problems of external adaptation and internal integration, that has worked well enough to be considered valid and, therefore, to be taught to new members as the correct way to perceive, think, and feel in relation to those problems."[3]

A more simplified working definition of organizational culture I like to use is how things get done within the organization when no one is watching. It is easy to focus on visible things when describing an organization's culture, such as things displayed in the hallways of the company office or how individuals in the company interact with each other. However, organizational culture consists of more than what can be observed. Culture consists of artifacts, values, and underlying assumptions.[4]

- **Artifacts:** The things you can see, feel, or hear in the workplace. Examples include what is displayed, office layouts, uniforms, identification badges, and topics discussed or not discussed.
- **Spoken Values:** What you are told and beliefs that you can use to make decisions. Examples include a company's vision and values or mission statement. These are explicitly stated official philosophies about the company.
- **Basic Assumptions:** Things that go without saying or are taken for granted. Examples could include speaking up in meetings, holding a door for someone, smiling or making eye contact, greeting someone by name when walking down the hall, and the degree of transparency with customers.

Often, many elements of an organization's culture are not visible daily and drop into the background—like how breathing is essential to life but not something we often consider until something interferes with our breathing. Significant events like a company merger or acquisition can make organizational cultural differences noticeable.

Individual and organizational development investments underperform without taking into consideration the influence of organizational culture. Companies that intentionally shape cultures supportive of leading with life-changing habits maximize their leadership development investments. Likewise, leaders attempting to break bad habits need to consider changing their environment and the culture of the organization when they lead to bring out their best outcomes.

• • •

Endnotes
1. Gregory, B., Harris, S., Armenakis, A., & Shook, C. (2009). "Organizational culture and effectiveness: A study of values, attitudes, and organizational outcomes." *Journal of Business Research*, 62(7), 673-679.
2. Cameron, K.S., & Quinn, R.E. (2011). "Diagnosing and Changing Organizational Culture: Based on the Competing Values Framework" (Third ed.). Jossey-Bass.
3. Schein, E., & Schein, P. (2016). *Organizational Culture and Leadership*, (5th ed.) John Wiley & Sons.
4. Ibid.

What are Worldview Forces and Why Are They Important?

Your worldview influences the way you think and how you make sense of the world around you. Today's dominant workplace worldview is that human reasoning reveals truth based on science, human reasoning, and objective evidence.[1] However, in recent years this way of thinking has brought into question if anything can be known with absolute certainty. It is an ideology of moral relativism that suggests everyone's values, beliefs, and claims to truth and lifestyles are equal. In response, business leaders encourage and promote tolerance. Yet because there is a belief that no absolute right or wrong exists, leaders are left feeling set up to fail when having to determine what makes for good ethical behavior and decisions. Leadership uncertainty in a crisis is dangerous because it slows down response times and creates confusion for leaders and followers, who don't know how to respond.

The Western culture of commercialism is based on excess and waste and fueled by low-cost, widely available, disposable products. This downward spiral of commoditization is contributing to some of the greatest economic, social, and environmental problems the global community faces. A moral relativism worldview has left decisions to be based on what is best for an individual's point of view. The contemporary world needs leaders who are inspired to create more than organizational efficiency and short-term gains. Products and services provided need to balance the desires of society/consumers and positively impact the planet, the organization's profit, and all people.

Technology, including artificial intelligence, is dramatically transforming the workplace in ways that rival how fire changed the world for Neanderthals. Advances in technology are further highlighting the limitations of moral relativism to guide ethical behavior. Because all values and beliefs are "truth," developers are uncertain how to program what are and are not morally acceptable decisions. Likewise, leaders are unsure about in what situations technology should be used as the final decision-maker. Modern challenges are amplifying the limitations of this dominant worldview and creating an opportunity for leaders to pursue something different . . . something not opposed to science, human reasoning, and objective evidence, but a worldview where we can have certainty in matters of people, profit, and purpose.

Answers to this dilemma are found through a spiritual lens. In other words, an understanding that God, who existed before the world, created the world out of nothing, and nothing exists outside of God's creation. This view is not opposed to science, objective evidence, or human reasoning, and it informs all aspects of work and life, providing absolute moral truth.

• • •

Endnotes
1. Kim, D., Fisher, D., & McCalman, D. (2009). "Modernism, Christianity, and Business Ethics: A Worldview Perspective." *Journal of Business Ethics*, Vol. 90 (1). pp. 115-12.

Why Effective Leadership Makes the Difference

Effective leadership makes a crucial difference in the personal and professional results you achieve and the life you live. If you have ever worked for a leader other than yourself, the statement that effective leadership makes a difference likely does not come as a surprise. Although no single definition for effective leadership exists, universal empirical research provides clear evidence that leadership moderates individual and organizational performance and makes a difference in the life of the leader, those they lead, and their impact on the world.

Good leadership can make a success out of a weak plan, but ineffective leadership can destroy a business that has a great strategic plan. According to a study of over two thousand businesses and leaders using a 360-degree survey, effective leadership accounted for a 38-percent increase in an organization's overall business performance. This same study then looked at the leadership effectiveness scores of the top and bottom performing 10 percent of companies. The results revealed that leadership effectiveness was at the 80th percentile in the top-performing companies. And leadership effectiveness was at the 30th percentile in the lowest-performing companies, lower than 70 percent of the norm leadership effectiveness scores.[1]

In the review and analysis of four separate studies in different industries on the impact of executive leadership transitions, it was discovered that leadership effectiveness could account for up to as much as 45 percent of an organization's performance.[2] According to Jim Collins in the book *Good to Great*,[3] a review of 1,435 companies studied over more than forty years revealed that leadership effectiveness accounted for up to 6.9 times greater returns than market averages.

Several research studies have investigated the connection between the leader and the followers' performance. A study of one hundred executives and middle management leaders in manufacturing and service organizations demonstrated that effective leadership improves follower performance and promotes higher business levels, follower job satisfaction, and follower organizational commitment.[4]

In addition to increased productivity of expected behavior, leadership impacts a follower's discretionary effort, also known as organizational citizenship behavior (OCB). Discretionary effort contributes to the bottom line beyond the formal job requirements of the follower. A study of 815 employees and 123 leaders found that effective leadership increases OCB and creates a workplace climate that benefits the organization.[5]

Fostering innovation within an organization is an increasingly important leadership behavior. It creates a competitive advantage in today's volatile, uncertain, complex, and ambiguous marketplace.[6] Executive leadership is essential for driving innovation. It influences both internal and external factors tied to organizational strategy and performance.[7]

Leadership trust is directly connected to employee retention, organizational commitment, and support for organizational change. According to the Edelman trust framework, trust is given based on competence and ethical behaviors. Similarly, in their book *The Leadership Challenge*, renowned authors James Kouzes and Barry Posner suggested that "credibility" is the foundation of leadership because employees must be able to trust their leaders.[8]

Leadership is a conversation. As air gives life to us, the words leaders speak can give life to a business. But words can also constrain and limit realities for individual employees, teams, and organizations. In a study of four hundred employees working in various companies with average company tenure of ten years, influential leaders increased two-way communication, creativity, collaboration, job attitudes, and organizational commitment.[9] The study provided evidence of how leadership communication cultivates quality leader-follower and employee-organization relationships.

• • •

Endnotes

1. Anderson, R., & Adams, W. (2016). *Mastering Leadership: An Integrated Framework for Breakthrough Performance and Extraordinary Business Results.* Wiley.
2. Day, D., & Lord, R. (1988). "Executive Leadership and Organizational Performance: Suggestions for a New Theory and Methodology." *Journal of Management*, 14(3), 453-464. https://doi.org/10.1177/014920638801400308
3. Collins, J. (2011). *Good to Great: Why Some Companies Make the Leap . . . and Others Don't.* Harper Business.
4. Dhar, U., & Mishra, P. (2001). "Leadership Effectiveness: A Study of Constituent Factors." *Journal of Management Research*, 1(4), 254.
5. Walumbwa, F., Hartnell, C., & Oke, A. (2010). "Servant Leadership, Procedural Justice Climate, Service Climate, Employee Attitudes, and Organizational Citizenship Behavior: A Cross-Level Investigation." *Journal of Applied Psychology*, 95, 517-529. https://doi.org/10.1037/a0018867
6. Eisenbeiss, S., van Knippenberg, D., & Boerner, S. (2008). "Transformational leadership and team innovation: Integrating team climate principles." *Journal of Applied Psychology*, 93(6), 1438-1446. doi:10.1037/a0012716
7. Zhang, H., Ou, A., Tsui, A., & Wang, H. (2017). "CEO humility, narcissism, and firm innovation: A paradox perspective on CEO traits." *The Leadership Quarterly*, 28(5), 585-604. doi:10.1016/j.leaqua.2017.01.003
8. Kouzes, J., & Posner, B. (2017). *The Leadership Challenge: How to Make Extraordinary Things Happen in Organizations* (Sixth ed.). Jossey-Bass.
9. Men, L. (2014). "Why Leadership Matters to Internal Communication: Linking Transformational Leadership, Symmetrical Communication, and Employee Outcomes." *Journal of Public Relations Research*, 26: 256–279.

What Are the 10 Worst Leadership Habits?

Leadership is one of the most researched and least understood topics in the social sciences. However, understanding what makes for outstanding leadership does not need to be complicated. Results and relationships are the true measures of a leader. Great leaders achieve success and significance in life and work by breaking the ten worst leadership habits (vices) listed here. To do that, leaders must build the life-changing habits (virtues) described for each one.

Bad Habit #1: Absence of Love for Followers. Great leaders selflessly love those they lead. Selfless love influences what a leader thinks and feels and shapes how he or she acts. Selfless love impacts every aspect of leadership.

Bad Habit #2: Failure to Consider What Might Be. Leaders who focus on what is wrong and ignore what might be limit what is possible. Words create worlds for both leaders and followers. Considering what might be creates alignment toward a shared vision and new possibilities.

Bad Habit #3: Lack of Data-Driven Decision-Making. Better decisions and taking the right actions requires modern leaders to embrace data-driven decision-making. Leaders who rely on stories without the proper analytics structure and organizational culture increase costs and fail to realize their organizations' full competitive advantage.

Bad Habit #4: Unintentional Leadership. Personal and professional success and significance are not accidents. Every leader gets the same amount of time in a day. Leaders who understand and maximize purpose not only know when to say yes, but, more importantly, when to say no—for both them and their team.

Bad Habit #5: Unbalanced Living. Achieving mental, physical, emotional, and spiritual balance enhances a leader's capacity. While time is a fixed part of every leader's equation, how the leader thinks, feels, and acts is a variable that influences the leader's performance and potential.

Bad Habit #6: Micro- and Macromanagement. Knowing when to be directive or to coach is essential for bringing out the best in followers. Excelling in management requires leaders to diagnose and engage with their followers appropriately—both individually and as a team. Too much or too little direction can increase stress and reduce productivity and creativity.

Bad Habit #7: Mismanaging Difficult Conversations. Leadership is a relationship. No relationship stays constant year-over-year, and mismanaging difficult conversations can lead to strife and missed growth opportunities. Leaders who master difficult conversations make the best change possible for individuals and their organizations.

Bad Habit #8: Absence of Trust. Trusting relationships create the most value. Unfortunately, leader-follower trust is becoming rarer in every organization. Trustworthy leaders are humble, reliable, credible, and transparent. Trust brings out the best in others by creating safety to engage in conflict.

Bad Habit #9: Fear of Failure. Innovation is increasingly important and dangerous for leaders. Organizations desire certainty, success, and efficiency. Yet uncertainty, failure, and inefficiency are sources of innovation. Many organizations are designed to keep leaders from taking risks. Embracing failure creates space for growth and innovation.

Bad Habit #10: Lack of Strategic Thinking. Many leaders and organizations do not possess the ability to change fast enough to avoid becoming obsolete. Identifying and understanding the drivers of change as they form enables strategic foresight where leaders are architects of change rather than managing reactions to change.

• • •

Two Important Questions

Before getting started with working on your leadership habits, you have two critical questions to consider.

Question #1: Do you want to change?
This may sound like an obvious question, given that you are reading a book on leading with life-changing habits. However, it is one thing to recognize a shortcoming and another to be entirely willing to take action to change these habits. This question gets to your mindset and willingness to make a change. Often your habits are comfortable ways of getting work done. Even though you know you are not getting the most out of life and work, you may not be entirely ready to give up what is comfortable.

I will relate this to my golf game. I've played since I was a child but began by holding the clubs incorrectly. This limited my distance and accuracy. Correctly holding the club felt awkward. When I changed to the proper grip, I found the ball went straighter but not as far as when I held the club incorrectly. I tried to break the habit, yet I'd sometimes resort to the old way of holding the club in high-pressure situations because it was comfortable.

Building life-changing habits and breaking the bad ones is not easy and requires being completely ready. If you are not sure you are entirely prepared to make a change, it is helpful to take an inventory. Ask yourself:

- What is at stake if you don't break the bad habit, and what is possible if you do? If you are unsure, you might find it helpful to talk with a coach or mentor.
- Write down the consequences and complications of the bad habit on both you and others.
- Ask yourself what feelings are associated with this bad habit.
- Reflect on what your leadership results and relationships could be like if you lead with the life-changing habit or do nothing.

Question #2: Is this a habit or an addiction?
Habits can lead to addictions, which can be more difficult to break. Habits are routines that get harder to give up the longer they go on. Addictions, on the other hand, are more challenging to break. When you are willing to sacrifice effectiveness to continue the behavior, you know you have an addiction. How is it that you can realize something is bad and still do it? Eating a jelly-filled donut is likely not a good idea when trying to lose weight. You know that telling your team to do something you are unwilling to do is a bad idea. So why keep doing it? And how do you stop?

As discussed in question number one, having the mindset and the willingness to change is helpful. Reading this book to learn about some transformative leadership skills is a good start. However, anyone who has tried to exercise more, lose weight, or permanently change any long-standing habit or addiction knows it can be challenging.

No one book, training event, or single coaching session will produce lasting behavioral change. That does not mean these are not helpful or important. It just means they need to be incorporated into a systemic change process to increase your odds of breaking an addiction. And if you are wondering, research does support that individuals without any bad habits are very rare, making the insights in this guide to leading with life-changing habits relevant, and an efficient part of your change process.

• • •

PART TWO

10 Life-Changing Habits

"Our greatest fear should not be of failure,
but of succeeding at things in life that don't really matter."
—FRANCIS CHAN[1]

Endnotes
1. Chan, F., & Yankoski, D. (2008). *Crazy Love: Overwhelmed by a Relentless God*. David C. Cook.

Life-Changing Habit #1
Loving Followers

> "To love is to will the good of the other."
> —ST. THOMAS AQUINAS[1]

OVERVIEW

Based on my experience and research on strategic leadership, there is no habit with more significant implications to a leader's success and significance than selfless love. Selfless love is a character strength that changes how a leader thinks, feels, and acts. While selfless love is rarely discussed in the context of leadership in the workplace, it influences everything.

Unfortunately, there is likely no other habit that is as rare in leadership. But this could be good news for you because it can be of great value to you and your followers, and perhaps lead to a tremendous competitive advantage for your business.

If selfless love is such a powerful tool for leaders, why is it so rarely practiced, or even discussed by businesses? There are several reasons. Many leaders don't fully understand the meaning of selfless love within the context of the workplace. Executives want their employees to like them, but love in reverse is something business schools rarely teach; it is not part of their thinking. Also, leaders don't establish expectations for themselves or others to love followers and don't receive rewards and recognition when they do. In fact, not too surprisingly, one of the first reactions I heard from talking with business leaders about this book was that they are not sure they want to love those they lead.

Defining Selfless Love

To understand the meaning of selfless love, it is helpful to examine the meaning of each word separately. To be "selfless" is to be more concerned with the needs and desires of others than with your own. If you believe your team needs to have a voice in a decision, but you are motivated not to bring it up to the team due to personal concern, you are not being selfless.

"Love" is one of those words in the English language with multiple meanings. One of the best definitions for love in the workplace comes from St. Thomas Aquinas, who stated that "To love is to will the good of the other." Putting these meanings together reveals that selfless love is putting desire and action for the good of others ahead of taking action in your interest.

While empathy, compassion, and selfless love are interrelated, they have distinct differences. Empathy is the ability to be aware of, feel and take on the emotions of what another person is experiencing. Empathy plays a vital role in moderating the effects of workplace conflict.[2] Research has linked empathy with forgiveness and healing relationships.[3] Compassion is an empathic understanding with a desire to help another person. Recent studies into the benefits of compassion at work link it to improvements in job performance, mental health, and leader-follower relationships.[4] Although having awareness (empathy) and a desire to help (compassion) is essential, the world needs leaders that put the desire for the good of others ahead of their own good. Leaders who emphasize selfless love bring out the best in how people think, act, and feel in the workplace—leading to personal and professional success and significance.[5]

VIRTUES OF LOVING FOLLOWERS

Three practical ways (virtues) to love followers are servant leadership, humility, and performance reinforcement.

Servant Leadership Style

Servant leadership is considered an emerging leadership style gaining global attention. Robert Greenleaf is considered by most researchers to be the founder of the modern servant leadership movement. He describes a servant leader as a servant first. "The best test, and difficult to administer, is: do those served grow as persons; do they, while being served, become healthier, wiser, freer, more autonomous, more likely themselves to become servants? And, what is the effect on the least privileged in society: will they benefit, or, at least, will they not be further deprived."[6]

Employees are looking for leaders who possess the following characteristics that are foundational to a servant leadership style[7]:

- listening to self and others
- empathy
- healing self and others
- awareness
- persuasion
- conceptual thinking
- foresight
- stewardship of others' needs
- commitment to people development
- building community

Understanding the characteristics employees seek does not fully capture servant leadership. Characteristics describe only what a leader should do in each situation. Leaders' virtues direct what they *will* do. Selfless love is identified as one of seven virtues that distinguish a servant leader.[8]

There are several proven individual and organizational benefits associated with servant leadership, including:

- performance
- productivity
- intrinsic motivation
- organizational citizenship behavior
- organizational alignment
- improved workplace climate
- enhanced employee capacity
- increased creativity

A servant leader's selfless love for others multiplies the benefits and outcomes of servant leadership and creates a better workplace. Increased leader and follower commitment increases intrinsic motivation, thus amplifying workforce alignment and business strategy. Intrinsic motivation is defined as doing a task for its inherent satisfaction rather than for another consequence.[9]

According to leading servant leadership expert Kathleen Patterson: "Higher levels of intrinsic motivation cause people to do more and results in higher performance."[10] Evidence shows that higher levels of intrinsic motivation result in higher employee productivity. One research study recommended that organizations should emphasize increased intrinsic motivation because, independent of a leader's style, it enhances employee engagement.

In addition to expected behavior, servant-leadership positively impacts an employee's discretionary effort, also known as organizational citizenship behavior (OCB).[11] Servant leadership improves the workplace climate and increases discretionary effort, which benefits an organization.

Humility

Humility is another virtue associated with a servant leadership style. Humble leaders are able to recognize their strengths and weaknesses.[12] They also appreciate others and believe that life is less about themselves and more about the greater good. Humble leadership is a balance between self-confidence and overconfidence; it is not a weak or indecisive approach to leadership. Humility is described as a personal desire to see oneself accurately, within perspective. In addition to these leadership behaviors, humility is linked with individual personality traits of conscientiousness, agreeableness, and openness.[13] Although associated, humble leaders do not always have strengths in each trait.

Humility creates space for leaders to listen, learn, and act. Intellectual humility enables leaders to present their ideas, demonstrate respect for other ideas, and be open to criticism. When leaders possess intercultural humility, it allows them to be open to different points of view on beliefs, values, and attitudes.[14]

After analyzing 1,435 companies over forty years, leadership guru Jim Collins concluded that humility and professional will are the most transformative executive leadership characteristics.[15] In a study involving ninety teams, leadership humility was demonstrated to enhance team innovation by cultivating an environment where employees feel safe to speak up about controversial points of view.[16] Across several research studies, humility is a demonstrated lever for sustainable company development, as well as enhancing employee innovation, team empowerment, company performance, and self-improvement.[17]

Reinforcing Worthy Performance

High performance is contagious.[18] Likewise, bringing out the best in followers brings out the best in the team. The potential of a team is greater than the sum of the individuals. Bringing out the best in followers requires purposeful performance reinforcement rather than managing poor performance. Every workplace is perfectly designed for followers to achieve the results the organization is currently getting, good or bad. Not all performance is worthy. Worthy performance results from employee behavior or action that leads to organizational benefit. A leader's role in reinforcing worthy performance goes beyond regular performance management tactics such as reviewing and conducting one-to-one meetings with employees.

The ABC model, also known as the three-contingency performance management model, provides a foundational understanding that helps leaders avoid costly or ineffective reinforcement mistakes.[19] The "A" stands for antecedents, which are anything that prompts behavior. Examples include work instructions, goals, objectives, targets, and job descriptions. The "B" stands for behavior or action, which is anything we say or do. The "C" stands for consequences, which are the results of the behavior or action. In the ABC model, consequences can increase or decrease behavior or action.

Antecedents	Behavior	Consequences
What prompts behavior	What we say and do	What happens as a result of behavior

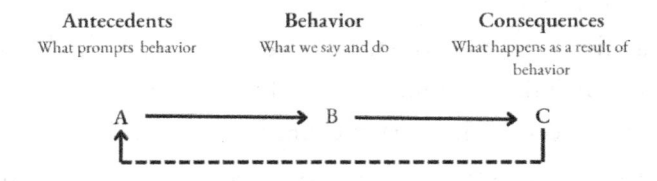

A ⟶ B ⟶ C

Figure adapted from Daniels and Daniels.[20]

Consequences have the most significant impact on influencing future behavior.[21] Consequences either increase or decrease desired behaviors. They are not all equal in their impact on behavior. The type, timing, and probability of a consequence influences the extent of its effect.

Consequences can be categorized by how they are experienced, timing, and probability. Consequences are either positive or negative as experienced by each follower. The timing of consequences is either immediate or future-oriented. The probability is either certain or uncertain. The strongest influences on behavior are the positive or negative consequences that occur while a behavior is happening. The weakest consequences are those delayed by more than a few seconds, with a low probability of occurring.

Performance reinforcement follows a behavior and increases the likelihood that the behavior will reoccur. Paying employees in advance of doing work is not performance reinforcement because it reinforces only the employee's promise to work. Reinforcement is inversely influenced by its frequency. The greater the frequency of the reinforcement, the lesser the impact on behavior recurrence.[22]

Effectively applying performance reinforcement leads to increased organizational citizenship behavior (OCB).[23] Also known as discretionary effort, OCB is performance management's "Holy Grail." It cracks the code of what is possible within a team and organization. Research studies have linked OCB with various positive individual and organizational outcomes, such as employee performance review ratings, compensation allocation, employee turnover intentions, absenteeism, operational efficiency, reduced costs, and customer satisfaction.

Discretionary effort is the level of performance employees might provide that goes above and beyond their formal job requirements for the organization's benefit. For example, imagine two retail stores' back-office employees walking down an aisle in their store. Both employees notice a piece of clothing on the floor. One employee stops to pick it up; the other walks around it. In this scenario, neither employee has the formal job description or responsibility for keeping the floors clear of clothing. It will, however, benefit the company if they pick up the piece of clothing. Discretionary effort is demonstrated by the employee picking up the piece of clothing and the organization realizing the benefit.

THE TRANSACTIONAL LEADER

Dan, a father of three young children, had aging parents. Life was a fast pace of balancing evening customer meetings, travel, children's events, and operations work. Dan was the new CEO of Transactional, a growing midsize company in the technology sector. Transactional was one of those quiet companies whose products are used in everyday life.

The daily pressures of a new executive role leading a growth-oriented company kept Dan rushing from meeting to meeting and second-guessing his priorities. Dan had risen through crucial leadership positions relatively quickly. To the employees at Transactional, Dan was known as the "golden boy" because everything he touched seemed to succeed. The organization had high hopes for continued growth and success with the transition of company leadership to Dan.

Through the constant pressures of his job and demands placed on his time, Dan stayed focused on the task at hand in every conversation. To survive, he felt compelled to get to the point in each conversation quickly. However, the harder Dan tried to advance the organization, the more demands were placed on his time, and his leadership team began to feel the pressure. Dan had inherited this team, and the team was beginning to feel more like consultants than employees.

To keep up with Dan, the team had to keep meetings focused on the specific project at hand, or their limited time with Dan would pass without them getting the input needed to meet their aggressive growth goals. Dan's team members were feeling disconnected and undervalued. However, they never mentioned it to Dan. The team didn't think Dan would care. Decisions were being made, the organization's balance sheet continued to grow, but the relationship problems were not presented to Dan.

Dan recognized that his relationships with his team members were not what they should be. To get more involvement, he decided to add additional meetings with each team member to his schedule. While the intent was to make time to listen to his team, Dan always felt like he was choosing between growing the company or growing the relationships with his team. Recognizing the growing percentage of time he was spending in meetings, Dan decided to mandate that all meetings be kept to 30 minutes or less without prior special request.

As a consequence, his leadership team added more meetings to get the needed time with Dan, and the team remained task-focused and increasingly disconnected from Dan and the company. Dan realized he was running from meeting to meeting. Sadly, he was still unaware of the growing concerns of his team.

The team at Transactional realized that regardless of what Dan would say in passing, they would be tasked only with his requests. They stopped offering ideas and focused on doing only what Dan requested. Dan got what he wanted, but the company started falling behind as decision quality decreased. Team members felt like no one had their backs. Transactional began to lose their best and brightest executives as they pursued opportunities to find success and significance in their lives.

While on the surface, the moral of this story appears to be about time management or meeting effectiveness, the more significant issue is the heart of the leader and the choices made in focusing on the team's heads and hands over winning their hearts.

Situations like this one between Dan and his team at Transactional are an unfortunate reality in many organizations. The biggest challenges on leaders' minds are change and growth in a volatile marketplace. Also, executive leaders often feel torn between success or significance. Dan gave up his ideas for personal significance by choosing to focus on organizational success.

EXAMPLES OF ABSENCE OF LOVE FOR FOLLOWERS

The bad habit of not loving followers can be recognized in transactional leaders when they display an absence of humility and tolerate poor performance.

Transactional Leadership

Leadership is a relationship, and people are the most significant resources within an organization. A transactional view of leadership adopts a top-down authoritarian view that organizational talent performs best within a chain of command that uses rewards and punishments to motivate and sees following the leader's directives as the employee's primary goal. It is a 'my-way-or-the-highway' leadership style.

Transactional leadership is centered around a paradigm in which leaders give employees something they want in exchange for getting something in return. Transactional leaders approach the workplace with the belief that most workers are not self-motivated and require structure, instruction, and monitoring to achieve organizational goals correctly and on time. Transactional leadership typically focuses on managing instead of leading and does not make substantial investments in building relationships with followers.

Example Attributes and Behaviors[24]

TRANSACTIONAL LEADERSHIP	SERVANT LEADERSHIP
• Top-down organizational structure	• Bottom-up organizational structure
• Employees need extrinsic motivation	• Employees need intrinsic motivation
• Change resistant	• Change resilient
• Linear thinking	• Cyclical thinking
• Efficiency solutions	• Holistic solutions

Absence of Humility (Narcissism)

The absence of humility is often considered narcissism, which is characterized by a highly self-involved personality, and a fragile ego susceptible to the faintest criticism. A narcissistic leader would tell you they don't care what you think unless it is positive about them. In a Cornell University study, narcissists were found to tend to support a hierarchical organizational structure if they are at the top or expect to get to the top.[25]

Narcissism is a proven predictor of counterproductive workplace behaviors such as sabotage, bullying, sexual harassment, fraud, employee theft, and absenteeism.[26] Alarmingly, research has demonstrated that narcissistic employees are likely to emerge as leaders in groups and teams that lack familiarity with one another.[27] Although organizational selection assessments can help identify narcissistic leaders, research has shown that followers often perceive narcissists as "good leaders."[28] Narcissistic individuals can project an image of effectiveness, even though they are viewed as arrogant.[29]

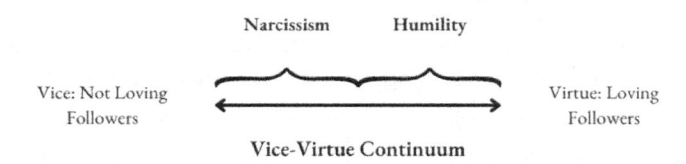

Vice: Not Loving Followers ← Narcissism | Humility → Virtue: Loving Followers

Vice-Virtue Continuum

Example Attributes and Behaviors

NARCISSISM	HUMILITY
• Inflated self-view	• Honest self-view
• The belief that they are superior	• Belief in a greater good
• Prefers personal recognition	• Prefers shared recognition
• Rejects negative feedback	• Seeks feedback to correct errors

Tolerating Poor Performance

Performance is contagious. When leaders tolerate poor performance, they reinforce poor performance by the individual and their entire team. When an employee's performance falls below the standards of the job, individuals, teams, and organizations suffer. A study revealed that underperforming employees average more than 15 percent of organizations.[30] Tolerating poor performance results in reduced productivity, poor-quality products and services, and team morale issues.[31] Poor performance results from gaps in the performer's behavior or the support of the individual's performance within the company.

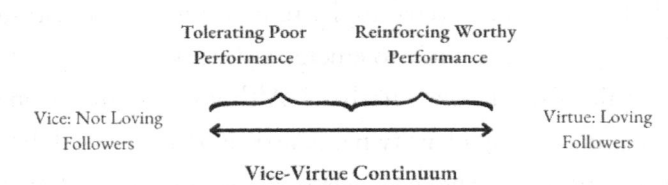

```
              Tolerating Poor    Reinforcing Worthy
              Performance         Performance
Vice: Not Loving   ←——————————→   Virtue: Loving
   Followers                         Followers
              Vice-Virtue Continuum
```

Example Attributes or Behaviors

TOLERATING POOR PERFORMANCE	REINFORCING PERFORMANCE
• Doesn't let performers know how they are underperforming	• Provides timely feedback for good performance
• Designs and provide tools without input from performers	• Asks others for information before making decisions
• Compensates poor performers the same as good performers	• Provides incentives for good performance
• Doesn't develop followers	• Invests in developing followers

LIFE-CHANGING HABIT #1: LOVING FOLLOWERS

Causes, Consequences & Complications of Absence of Love for Followers

- Low-Quality Relationships
- Increased Employee Turnover
- Stalling Career
- Decreased Employee Engagement
- Limited Creativity
- Increased Counter-Productive Behaviors
- Lack of Committed Followers
- Decreased Team Cohesion

Absence of Love for Followers (Personal | Professional)

Selfless love is rare in leadership. It is not easy to achieve selfless love, even when expectations are clear, and the leader understands what needs to be done. Both environmental and individual factors contribute to the absence of selfless love in the workplace. Often, attention is given to rewarding personal interests rather than a desire to act for the good of another. Common causes include: (1) a lack of attentiveness to expectations for leaders to demonstrate selfless love for followers; (2) a lack of feedback for leaders; (3) a lack of selfless love understanding and skills; (4) a lack of selection processes to identify potential leaders with intrinsic values aligned with selfless love; and (5) a lack of incentives for leaders to practice selfless love within the organization.

Some argue that selfless love is not possible within a business because economics force individuals to be motivated on some level by self-interest. Numerous philosophical, political, economic, and biological arguments have been made challenging the existence of pure selfless love.[32] However, applying available measurements of selfless love reveals a typical bell curve between individuals in solid agreement and those in strong disagreement.

Complications arising from leaders not loving workplace followers are often disguised as low employee engagement, reduced team morale, meager team cohesion or collaboration, increased employee turnover, poor-quality products and services, rising counterproductive workplace behaviors, and failed execution.[33]

TRANSFORMATIONAL TOOLS & EXERCISES FOR LOVING FOLLOWERS

How to Measure Servant Leadership. The following servant-leadership 360 evaluation, adapted from research by Bruce Winston, director of the Ph.D. in Organizational Leadership program for Regent University, and Dail Fields, the Senior Research Scientist with the Institute for Behavioral Research at the University of Georgia, identify the core behaviors that make servant-leadership work at all levels of leadership.[34] The ten behaviors listed below represent the minimum number of items to adequately evaluate servant-leadership as described initially by Greenleaf:[35]

1. Practices what they preach
2. Serves people without regard to their nationality, gender, or race
3. Sees serving as a mission of responsibility to others
4. Is genuinely interested in employees as people
5. Understands that serving others is most important
6. Is willing to make sacrifices to help others
7. Seeks to instill trust rather than fear or insecurity
8. Is always honest
9. Is driven by a sense of higher calling

10. Promotes values that transcend self-interest and material success

For additional recommendations on keys to 360-degree assessment success, you will want to read the chapter on maximizing purpose.

How to Measure Your Humility. The Character Strengths Survey from the VIA Institute on Character is a useful tool for defining a leader's values. The free VIA Character Strength Survey provides insights into twenty-four character strengths, including humility, in rank order. According to the VIA Institute on Character, humility falls within the virtue category of temperance, which relates to how a leader manages habits. Character strengths are values in action or positive traits for thinking, feeling, and behaving that benefit the leader and others. The VIA has been completed by over 15 million people globally, and all the scales have satisfactory reliability. While knowing where you are is essential, it is likely more important to know where you are going. For more information regarding the VIA Character Strengths Survey, please go to www.viacharacter.org.

How to Understand Performance Consequences. Applying consequence analysis to the workplace is a great way to learn more about actions and reactions and what can be done to reinforce performance.[36] The first step is to clarify the desired behavior and who is the target of the analysis. This step is critical to quality. When completing the analysis, it is vital to concentrate on the desired behavior being assessed and to remain focused on the consequences from the performer's point of view. The second step is to identify all the antecedents and consequences for the desired behavior. Assess if the consequences are positive or negative, occur immediately or in the future, and are certain or uncertain as experienced by the performer. The performer's world is perfectly designed to get the results they are getting. It is unlikely that the performer will perform the desired behavior when more impactful reinforcement exists for the undesired behavior.

How to Optimize Performance Controls: Environmental and individual performance factors optimize performance. Skills and knowledge, capacity, and motivation are factors the performer controls. Information, tools, resources, and incentives are factors the leader influences. The six aspects are described below in the Behavior Engineering Model created by Thomas Gilbert. You can use the model to understand what you need to optimize your performance and uncover what your followers need to improve their performance on any given task. When using this to diagnose opportunities for improvement, a simple way to get started is to ask which one of these areas would help you improve most.

The Behavior Engineering Model[37]

ENVIRONMENT		
Information	**Tools & Resources**	**Incentives**
• Relevant and frequent feedback about performance, clear expectations, clear guides to acceptable performance	• Tools, resources, time, and materials of work designed to match performance requirements	• Financial and non-financial career development opportunities and consequences for poor performance

INDIVIDUAL		
Skill & Knowledge	**Capacity**	**Motivation**
• Basic/specialized understanding of concepts, theories, system construction, fundamentals, and skills	• Physical, mental, and emotional factors influencing an individual's ability/capacity to perform a job or task	• Intrinsic & induced motivation related to an individual's needs for achievement, affiliation, security, and control

KEY POINTS—LOVING FOLLOWERS

- Selfless love is a character strength that changes how a leader thinks, feels, and acts.
- Selfless love in leadership is to desire and act for the good of another, ahead of your own interest.
- Employees are looking for leaders to follow that possess the characteristics foundational to a servant leadership style.
- Selfless love for others multiplies benefits associated with servant leadership.
- Humility creates space for leaders to listen and learn intellectually and interculturally and accept and implement employee suggestions.
- Humility is one of the most transformative executive leadership characteristics.
- Performance is contagious, and bringing out the best in followers brings out the best in teams.
- The strongest influences on behavior are the consequences that occur while the behavior is happening.

REFLECTION QUESTIONS—LOVING FOLLOWERS

- What greater life purpose do you care enough about to take a stand for?
- Do you have the will to love those you lead?
- What do your followers need most?
- Are those you are leading growing, serving others, and prepared to surpass you?
- Do you take time to connect with those who follow you?
- How well do you know how those you lead spend their time and money outside of work?

- How well does your self-assessment of your performance align with how others view your accomplishments?
- On a scale of 1–10, how would you assess how you are doing with loving followers?
- Where are your most significant growth opportunities?

• • •

Endnotes

1. Gallagher, D. (1999). "Thomas Aquinas on Self-Love as the Basis for Love of Others." *Acta Philosophica,* 8(1):23-44.
2. Ran, Y., Liu, Q., Cheng, Q., & Zhang, Y. (2021). "Implicit-explicit power motives congruence and forgiveness in the workplace conflict: the mediating role of empathy." *The International Journal of Conflict Management,* 32(3), 445-468. https://doi.org/10.1108/IJCMA-06-2020-0116
3. McCullough, M., Worthington, E., & Rachal, K. (1997). "Interpersonal forgiving in close relationships". *Journal of Personality and Social Psychology,* 73(2), 321–336. https://doi.org/10.1037/0022-3514.73.2.321
4. Chu, L. (2017). "Impact of Providing Compassion on Job Performance and Mental Health: The Moderating Effect of Interpersonal Relationship Quality." *Journal of Nursing Scholarship,* 49(4), 456-465. https://doi.org/10.1111/jnu.12307
5. Ferris, R. (1988). "How organizational love can improve leadership." *Organizational Dynamics,* 16(4), 40.
6. Greenleaf, R., & Spears, L. (2002). *Servant Leadership: A Journey into the Nature of Legitimate Power and Greatness* (25th-anniversary ed.). Paulist Press.
7. Spears, L. C. (1998). "Servant Leadership." *Executive Excellence,* 15(7), 11.
8. Patterson, K. (2003). "Servant Leadership—A Theoretical Model" [PDF]. Regent University School of Leadership Studies Servant leadership Research Roundtable.
9. Oudeyer, P., & Kaplan, F. (2007). "What is intrinsic motivation? A typology of computational approaches." *Frontiers in Neurorobotics,* 1, 6-6. https://doi.org/10.3389/neuro.12.006.2007
10. Patterson, K. (2003). "Servant Leadership—A Theoretical Model" [PDF]. Regent University School of Leadership Studies Servant leadership Research Roundtable.
11. Walumbwa, F., Hartnell, C., & Oke, A. (2010). "Servant Leadership, Procedural Justice Climate, Service Climate, Employee Attitudes, and Organizational Citizenship Behavior: A Cross-Level Investigation." *Journal of Applied Psychology,* 95(3).

12. Ou, A., Waldman, D., & Peterson, S. (2018). "Do Humble CEOs Matter? An Examination of CEO Humility and Firm Outcomes." *Journal of Management, 44*(3), 1147–1173.
13. Morris, J., Brotheridge, C., & Urbanski, J. (2005). "Bringing humility to leadership: Antecedents and consequences of leader humility." *Human Relations*, 58(10), 1323-1350. Retrieved from http://eres.regent.edu/login?url=https://www-proquest-com.ezproxy.regent.edu/scholarly-journals/bringing-humility-leadership-antecedent/docview/231523313/se-2?accountid=13479
14. Van Tongeren, D., Davis, D., Hook, J., & Witvliet, C. (2019). "Humility." *Current Directions in Psychological Science: A Journal of the American Psychological Society, 28*(5), 463-468. https://doi.org/10.1177/0963721419850153
15. Collins, J. (2001). *Good to Great: Why Some Companies Make the Leap . . . and Others Don't.* Harper Business.
16. Ou, A., Waldman, D., & Peterson, S. (2018). "Do Humble CEOs Matter? An Examination of CEO Humility and Firm Outcomes." *Journal of Management, 44*(3), 1147–1173.
17. Ren, Q., Xu, Y., Zhou, R., & Liu, J. (2020). "Can CEO's Humble Leadership Behavior Really Improve Enterprise Performance and Sustainability? A Case Study of Chinese Start-Up Companies." *Sustainability, 12*(8), 3168.
18. de Jong, B., Bijlsma-Frankema, K., & Cardinal, L. (2014). "Stronger Than the Sum of Its Parts? The Performance Implications of Peer Control Combinations in Teams." *Organization Science*, 25(6), 1703-1721. https://doi.org/10.1287/orsc.2014.0926
19. Weatherly, N., & Malott, R. (2008). "An Analysis of Organizational Behavior Management Research in Terms of the Three-Contingency Model of Performance Management." *Journal of Organizational Behavior Management*, 28(4), 260-285. https://doi.org/10.1080/01608060802454643
20. Daniels, A., & Daniels, J. (2004). *Performance Management: Changing Behavior that Drives Organizational Effectiveness (Fourth ed.).* Performance Management Publications.
21. ibid.
22. ibid.
23. ibid.
24. Trompenaars, A., & Voerman, E. (2009). *Servant-Leadership Across Cultures: Harnessing the Strength of the World's Most Powerful Management Philosophy.* McGraw Hill.

25. Zitek, E., & Jordan, A. (2016). "Narcissism Predicts Support for Hierarchy (At Least When Narcissists Think They Can Rise to the Top.)" *Social Psychological and Personality Science*, 7(7), 707–716.
26. Brender-Ilan, Y., & Sheaffer, Z. (2019). "How do self-efficacy, narcissism and autonomy mediate the link between destructive leadership and counterproductive work behaviour." *Asia Pacific Management Review*, 24(3), 212-222. https://doi.org/10.1016/j.apmrv.2018.05.003
27. Brunell, A., Gentry, W. Campbell, W., Hoffman, B., Kuhnert, K., & DeMarree, K. (2008). "Leader emergence: The case of the narcissistic leader." *Personality and Social Psychology Bulletin*, 34(12), 1663-1676.
28. ibid.
29. Nevicka, B., Ten Velden, F., De Hoogh, A., & Van Vianen, A. (2011). "Reality at odds with perceptions: Narcissistic leaders and group performance." *Psychological Science*. 22(10):1259-1264. doi:10.1177/0956797611417259
30. Faragher, J. (2006). "Employers lose £32m a year, tolerating poor performance." *Personnel Today*, 1.
31. Plump, C. (2010). "Dealing with problem employees: A legal guide for employers." *Business Horizons*, 53(6), 607-618. https://doi.org/10.1016/j.bushor.2010.07.003
32. Wilson, D. (2015). *Does Altruism Exist?: Culture, Genes, and the Welfare of Others*. Yale University Press.
33. Brender-Ilan, Y., & Sheaffer, Z. (2019). "How do self-efficacy, narcissism and autonomy mediate the link between destructive leadership and counterproductive work behaviour." *Asia Pacific Management Review*, 24(3), 212-222. https://doi.org/10.1016/j.apmrv.2018.05.003 Plump, C. M. (2010). "Dealing with problem employees: A legal guide for employers." *Business Horizons*, 53(6), 607-618. https://doi.org/10.1016/j.bushor.2010.07.003
34. Winston, B., & Fields, D. (2015). "Seeking and measuring the essential behaviors of servant leadership." *Leadership & Organization Development Journal*, 36(4), 413-434.
35. Greenleaf, R., & Spears, L. (2002). *Servant Leadership: A Journey into the Nature of Legitimate Power & Greatness* (25th Anniversary ed.). Paulist Press.
36. Daniels, A., & Daniels, J. (2006). *Performance Management: Changing Behavior that Drives Organizational Effectiveness*. Performance Management Publications.
37. Gilbert, T. (1978). *Human Competence: Engineering Worthy Performance*. McGraw-Hill.

Life Changing Habit #2
Focusing on Strengths

"The ageless essence of leadership is to create an alignment of strengths, in ways which make a system's weaknesses irrelevant."
—PETER DRUCKER[1]

OVERVIEW

Communication is one of the most central functions of life.[2] Words shape perceptions of the workplace.[3] Focusing on strengths unlocks "what might be" for individuals, teams, and organizations.

In most businesses, workdays are typically filled with finding and fixing problems. It is easy to focus on what is wrong and never provide the time or space to discuss what is right. This kind of workplace environment makes it a challenge for leaders to focus on strengths. In many organizations, leaders operate as firefighters. They are putting out one fire after the next. The results are incremental improvements and efficiency. A high hidden cost is a distraction from pursuing innovation and the best of what can be.

Additionally, when leaders are always approaching employees about what is wrong, eventually, they don't want to see that leader anymore, even if what they have to share is helpful. They can become conditioned to associate problems in the workplace with the leader. You know this link has occurred when leaders feel obligated to say, "I am here to help." They are saying this because they know they are not being viewed that way.

Strengths are expected and taken for granted. Many leaders adopt the point of view that they pay employees for their best work, and that is enough. Often leaders underestimate the need and miss the opportunity for rewarding and recognizing what is desired and expected.

Defining a Strengths-Focus

Let's define strength as the best of what is, and the potential for the best of what can be within a person, team, or organization. Having a strengths-focus is not about ignoring weaknesses but about prioritizing and pursuing understanding and reinforcing and leveraging strengths.

VIRTUES OF FOCUSING ON STRENGTHS

Two practical ways (virtues) to focus on strengths are reward and recognition, and strengths thinking.

Reward and Recognition

Reward and recognition processes are powerful leadership tools. When properly designed and applied, they increase desired behaviors and shape the workplace culture for both individuals and teams, either co-located or geographically dispersed.[4] Recognition is a symbolic gesture of appreciation for the desired achievement. Common workplace examples include thank-you notes, plaques, team celebrations, and letters of commendation. In behavioral science terms, recognition is a form of social reinforcement. A reward is a tangible form of support for desired results. The most common reward in the workplace is money, either in a bonus or one-time spot reward. Unfortunately,

LIFE-CHANGING HABIT #2: FOCUSING ON STRENGTHS

when reward and recognition systems are incorrectly designed and applied, they fail to motivate employees and, worse, make people unhappy.

Should leaders provide rewards and recognition? Not every leader agrees that reward and recognition systems are helpful. Some leaders voice concern over giving rewards and recognition for behaviors that are expected to be done.

Effective reward and recognition systems are:

- Targeted toward specific behaviors
- Applied immediately or frequently
- Customized to what the individual values
- Focused on what is achieved and how it is achieved
- Able to present everyone with the same opportunity to achieve the reward or recognition[5]

Effective reward and recognition systems increase desired behaviors. Leaders can measure the effectiveness of the applied reward or recognition by measuring if the desired behavior increases.

Strengths Thinking

Many current work processes are designed to identify weaknesses rather than find strengths. However, an emerging trend within businesses is to adopt strengths-based thinking over a traditional problem or deficit-oriented view.[6] Strengths at an individual level are favorable traits and what people do best and enjoy. The more a strength is used, the stronger it becomes.[7]

Leaders adopting a strengths-thinking approach versus a deficit focus achieved an 86 percent greater probability of success.[8] When employees are doing what they do best, it leads to higher levels of engagement, well-being at work, and productivity.[9]

Too often, leaders begin and end the workday approaching business challenges from the point of view of fixing what is wrong. Taking a strength approach considers a balance regarding strengths and weaknesses.[10] It is imperative to fix problems. However, leaders miss the opportunity to engage in inspiring work and realize shared dreams when time is not spent thinking and discussing challenges in the context of what is possible.

Appreciative Inquiry (AI) is an organizational development approach based on the understanding that by committing to solving challenges through discerning the best of what is, and what might be, transformational[11] new realities are created.[12]

A few basic assumptions of AI are:

- Words shape worlds
- People attain greater confidence to make changes building on the best of the past
- Individuals, teams, and organizations move in the direction discussed
- Questions create influence
- In every person, team, or organization, something is already good and works

This appreciative approach follows a four "D" process:[13]

1. Discovery—finding the best of what is
2. Dream—collaborating on the best of what can be
3. Design—establishing creative strategies to move from what is to what can be
4. Destiny—executing the design strategies with excellence and revising as needed

Like most problem-solving processes, AI starts with identifying a team of core stakeholders. However, before you can move to discovery,

LIFE-CHANGING HABIT #2: FOCUSING ON STRENGTHS

you need to use the stakeholder team to determine the focal point. The focal point is framed positively, such as embracing diversity, equity, and inclusion in the workplace instead of decreasing diverse employee turnover. Once the focal point is crafted, appreciative questions are presented to as many stakeholders as possible to reveal the current state's best from those closest to the work.

Next, the team phrases the vision and images of the dream into aspiration statements. Themes developed from the discovery and dream stages result in action-oriented steps toward the aspirational statements. Goals and action steps taken are reviewed in the destiny phase to ensure the changes are appropriately incorporated into everyday life.

THE PROBLEM

Mario was a mid-level manager within a midsize healthcare organization. He had worked hard for his company for seven years in the role he was initially recruited for, director of marketing. Before joining Mid-Astra, Mario was the CEO of a small business involved in sales. The small business did very well and was bought by Mid-Astra. Mario decided to join Mid-Astra, thinking it was a chance to learn from others with more significant potential and stability. Mario was a natural within marketing and sales. His current employer, Mid-Astra, was growing from being a local provider to a regional health services organization.

Mario and his team worked hard to get results. Over his seven years with Mid-Astra, he had several significant accomplishments. Mario found his work fulfilling, and he was hopeful he would be considered for a future vice president role. Mario was a little concerned because the past couple of opportunities had been filled with outside talent. Mario's team was always in transition. New hires would join his team and then move to other departments within a couple of years. Mario thought of himself as a talent for developing new hires.

Mario viewed the world as a problem needing to be solved. He could spot what was wrong in a project and continuously make improvements. Mario's ability to spot what was wrong was both a blessing and a curse. He was not aware that he was considered within Mid-Astra as difficult to work with and for. People knew that when they worked with Mario, they would be made aware of problems and weaknesses needing to be fixed. His leader, Cheryl, vice president of sales and marketing, liked the results Mario and his team could achieve. Also, the CEO of Mid-Astra gave Mario and his team company awards for their accomplishments. Mario believed people learn best by jumping in the deep end of the pool. It is either "sink or swim," he would say.

Mario could never find a successor for his role. It seemed like when someone with the talent to match his joined the team, they would leave for another career opportunity.

In a recent conversation with Cheryl, Mario learned that he was not being considered for an upcoming new VP role. Mario was disappointed. He thought she would recognize his efforts to develop talent and that the CEO awards validated his ability. When Mario questioned Cheryl, he received feedback that he was not viewed as a great developer of people. This came as a big surprise to Mario because it was the first time he had received this feedback in seven years.

He immediately became defensive and used examples of employees he had hired onto his team that had moved on to new roles within the organization. Mario's leader avoided giving him the feedback he needed because she didn't want to lose Mario from Mid-Astra and suggested he needed to develop a successor.

Mario left this meeting hearing that he needed to challenge his team to grow more than he had in the past, or he would likely not be considered for future VP roles within the organization. Mario decided to continue providing critical feedback to his team on improving and challenging them with demanding assignments.

LIFE-CHANGING HABIT #2: FOCUSING ON STRENGTHS

Over the following months and years, Mario became further frustrated, and his team morale began to decline. Mario had become more challenging to work for, and his team turnover had increased. Now, with an increasingly difficult hiring market, Mario was always short-staffed.

Mario eventually left Mid-Astra feeling like he'd wasted a few years of his career. He never connected the impact of his approach with the outcome of the situation. Mid-Astra, however, continued growing and is pursuing becoming a national player in the health services industry.

Not getting all the feedback you need the higher you go in an organization is too familiar for leaders with good results. Mario possessed some exceptional talent as a marketing leader, talent that made him essential to the team. Unfortunately, those same qualities prevented him from receiving the feedback he needed to hear.

One takeaway from this story could be the importance of leaders getting honest feedback. Another, however, is that when leaders see people as needing to be fixed, it negatively impacts relationships and constrains what might be. Also, development is not throwing team members into situations they aren't prepared to handle and watching to see if they "sink or swim."

EXAMPLES OF FAILURE TO CONSIDER WHAT MIGHT BE

The bad habit of failing to see what might be in the workplace can be recognized by a leader's improper use of negative reinforcement and an overemphasis on deficit thinking.

Negative Reinforcement

What happens in the workplace results from either positive or negative forms of reinforcement. Where positive reinforcement increases performance beyond expectations, negative reinforcement results in compliance with expectations. A level of performance to escape or avoid an undesirable consequence.[14] When a leader declares, "If you do not achieve your performance goals, I will have to let you go" or "If your performance does not improve, you need to attend an early-morning training meeting," these are forms of negative reinforcement. One reason for negative reinforcement in the workplace is that it elicits an immediate observable action. However, this approach's unseen, hidden costs are the difference between a minimum level of compliance and the breakthrough potential of what is possible.

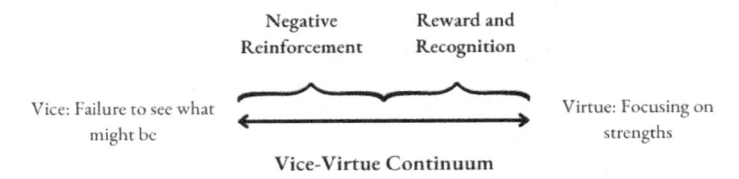

```
                    Negative        Reward and
                  Reinforcement     Recognition

Vice: Failure to see what  ⟵─────────────⟶   Virtue: Focusing on
      might be                                      strengths
                        Vice-Virtue Continuum
```

Example Attributes and Behaviors

NEGATIVE REINFORCEMENT	REWARD AND RECOGNITION
• Compliance	• Commitment
• Looking for what is wrong	• Looking for what is right
• Threatening employees	• Praising employees

Deficit Thinking

A deficit-thinking approach starts with leaders identifying shortcomings and then selecting solutions to improve those shortcomings. The goal is to find all the potential gaps so that continuous improvements can be made. While this approach leads to incremental progress, it does not unlock growth beyond knowing the solution to the problem. Deficit-thinking leadership approaches fail businesses and communities. This thinking has led to incremental workplace improvements, a flood of low-cost, high-quality disposable products, and a lack of innovation.[15]

LIFE-CHANGING HABIT #2: FOCUSING ON STRENGTHS

While deficit-thinking approaches have been used successfully, they are not without risks. Deficit-thinking techniques put people on the defensive and, in some cases, shape a culture of blame.

Compared with strengths-based approaches, deficit-oriented thinking leads to lower employee engagement, lower levels of performance improvement, and higher employee attrition rates. In education, studies found that students engaged in approaches that identified weaknesses had lower perceptions of their competence and lower intrinsic motivation to learn.[16] Additionally, they expended less effort to learn than when strength-based approaches were used.[17]

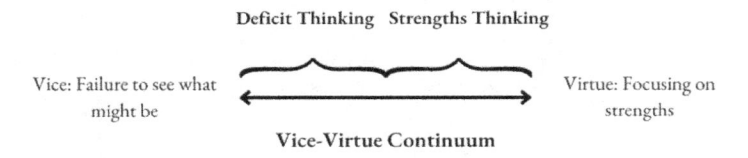

Deficit Thinking   Strengths Thinking

Vice: Failure to see what might be ⟷ Virtue: Focusing on strengths

Vice-Virtue Continuum

Example Attributes and Behaviors

DEFICIT THINKING	STRENGTHS THINKING
• What is wrong or missing	• The best of what is and can be
• Predict and control	• Discover and adapt
• Efficiency	• Design
• Crisis	• Opportunity

CAUSES, CONSEQUENCES & COMPLICATIONS OF FAILURE TO CONSIDER WHAT MIGHT BE

Lack of Commitment

Compliance Mindset

Lower Levels of Effort

Failure to Consider What Might Be
Personal | Professional

Decreased Employee Engagement

Lack of Intrinsic Motivation to Learn

Decreased Performance

Lower Perception of Competence

Higher Attrition Rates

Most businesses are designed to encourage leaders to develop the bad habit of failing to consider what might be. A leader's typical workday is filled with finding what is wrong. It is easier to recognize a problem that arises than to recognize when something is not fulfilling what is possible.

Many organizations value leaders who solve problems—and for a good reason. Problems result in negative impacts on effectiveness or efficiency. Typically, problem-solving leaders receive thank-you notes or recognition from critical stakeholders such as employees, customers, or their leader for bringing solutions to these business pain points.

When leaders use negative reinforcement, they can see an immediate behavior change. Negative reinforcement is an easy way out but misses the greater potential. This positive reinforcement for the leader increases the likelihood of the leader continuing to use negative reinforcement.

LIFE-CHANGING HABIT #2: FOCUSING ON STRENGTHS

When leaders use reward and recognition to bring out the best in their employees, there is a delay until the employee performs the desired behavior before the leader will see if their positive reinforcement was effective.

The complications that arise from failing to consider what might be in the workplace include compliance to what is expected and monitored versus commitment and discretionary effort.[18] Additional complications include lower employee engagement, lower levels of performance improvement, and higher employee attrition rates.[19] A failure to consider what is possible within individuals lowers their perceptions of competence, intrinsic motivation to learn, and expended lower levels of effort.[20]

TRANSFORMATIONAL TOOLS & EXERCISES FOR FOCUSING ON STRENGTHS

How to Improve Reward and Recognition. When choosing good low-cost rewards and recognition for employees, it is helpful to know your team. Don't give others what *you* want. Give others what *they* want. Platinum Rule: Do unto others as they would like to be done unto them. A reinforcement survey is an efficient and effective way to identify these potential reinforcers. The following survey questions can be used to get to know your team. In one-to-one meetings explore what employees spend their time and resources outside of work.[21]

- What hobbies do you spend time and money doing?
- What music do you enjoy listening to?
- What concerts do you attend?
- What sports do you watch?
- What sports do you play?
- What do you enjoy reading?
- What movies do you enjoy watching?
- What social events do you enjoy attending?
- Do you enjoy singing?

- Do you enjoy dancing?
- Do you enjoy playing a musical instrument? If so, which one(s)?
- Do you enjoy shopping? If so, what store(s)?
- Do you enjoy cooking? If so, what?
- Do you enjoy painting?
- What other things do you enjoy spending time and money doing?

Once you understand your employees better, you can customize your reinforcement and then observe to ensure they find it reinforcing. Remember that adults prefer variety and to adjust your support over time.

How to Use Appreciative Framing. Individuals, teams, and organizations move in the direction repeatedly discussed, and questions are asked. Appreciative Inquiry assumes that the inquiries define outcomes and influence the results by discussing them. Appreciative framing is taking a given focal point for transformation and restating it as an opportunity. The following are some examples:

FRAMED AS CONCERNS	FRAMED AS OPPORTUNITIES
• Bias in the workplace	• Embracing differences at work
• Customer complaints	• Exceptional customer support
• Missed opportunities	• Seeing new challenges
• Absence of leadership	• Growing exceptional leaders

How to Facilitate Appreciative Interviews. Every individual and team has strengths. In contrast to problem-solving, focus on what has worked, what is working, and strengths. An appropriately developed appreciative interview builds on these points to guide the individual and team toward a positive future. Once the focal point of the discussion is framed appropriately and appreciatively, the following are a couple of helpful appreciative questions to use:

LIFE-CHANGING HABIT #2: FOCUSING ON STRENGTHS

- What would you wish for if you had three wishes to dramatically improve your organization's health and vitality? (And no, you cannot wish for more wishes.)
- Imagine it is five years from today, and everything you had wished for and hoped for related to the appreciative focal point of the interview has come true. What would you see and hear? Describe the changes with people, processes, places, products, and services. Describe what you or others have done to make these changes possible.

Then focus on the positive things happening, how they are happening, and what attributes make their dreams and wishes so exciting.

How to Identify Your Strengths. Based on my experiences and review of the reliability and validity literature, the VIA Character Strengths Survey and the Clifton StrengthsFinder Assessment are two of the most scientifically backed and relatively low-cost quantitative strength-based assessments. These assessments can be completed online and provide development recommendations and support materials.

The VIA Character Strengths Survey is a valuable tool for defining a leader's strengths as values. The free VIA Character Strength Survey provides insights into your twenty-four character strengths in rank order. Character strengths are values in action or positive traits for thinking, feeling, and behaving that benefit the leader and others. The VIA has been completed by over 15 million people globally, and all the scales have satisfactory reliability (> 0.70 alphas). For more information regarding the VIA Character Strengths Survey, please go to www.viacharacter.org.

The CliftonStrengths Assessment can be a helpful tool for identifying your top strengths and providing a shared vocabulary for the thirty-four CliftonStrengths themes. There is solid evidence to support the benefit of this assessment combined with strengths-based development programs that demonstrate performance improvement.[22] For more information regarding the CliftonStrengths Assessment, please go to www.gallup.com/cliftonstrengths/en/253850/cliftonstrengths-for-individuals.aspx. Also, for a free code to complete the assessment and learn more, you should read *StrengthsFinder 2.0* by Tom Rath.[23]

KEY POINTS—FOCUSING ON STRENGTHS

- Many current work processes are designed to identify weaknesses rather than discover strengths.
- Having a strengths-focus is not about ignoring weaknesses but prioritizing and pursuing understanding, reinforcing, and leveraging strengths.
- Words shape perceptions within the workplace.
- A high hidden cost of failing to focus on strengths is a distraction from pursuing the best of what can be and a lack of innovation.
- When properly designed and applied, reward and recognition increase desired behaviors and shape the workplace culture for individuals and teams, regardless of location.
- Strength is the best of what is and the potential for the best within a person, team, or organization.

REFLECTION QUESTIONS—FOCUSING ON STRENGTHS

- What are your personal and professional dreams? If everything you hoped for and wished for came true, describe what you would see, what you would be doing, and where you would be doing it.
- What do you enjoy doing most? Where do you enjoy spending your time?
- How do you feel when listening to others talk about their dreams?
- What is important to those you lead?
- Describe a few times or projects when you were at your best. What is an emerging theme you can learn from those experiences about when you are at your best?

• • •

LIFE-CHANGING HABIT #2: FOCUSING ON STRENGTHS

Endnotes

1. Whitney, D., & Trosten-Bloom, A. (2003). *The Power of Appreciative Inquiry: A Practical Guide to Positive Change.* Berrett-Koehler Publishers.
2. Greenaway, K., Wright, R., Willingham, J., Reynolds, K., & Haslam, S. (2015). "Shared Identity Is Key to Effective Communication." *Personality and Social Psychology Bulletin*, 41(2), 171–182. https://doi.org/10.1177/0146167214559709
3. Wolff, P., & Holmes, K. (2011). "Linguistic relativity." Wiley Interdisciplinary Reviews. *Cognitive Science*, 2(3), 253-265. https://doi.org/10.1002/wcs.104
4. Ng, P., & Tung, B. (2018). "The importance of reward and recognition system in the leadership of virtual project teams: A qualitative research for the financial services sector." *Journal of Transnational Management, 23*(4), 198-214. https://doi.org/10.1080/15475778.2018.1512827
5. Daniels, A. (2016). *Bringing Out the Best in People: How to Apply the Astonishing Power of Positive Reinforcement* (3rd edition). McGraw Hill.
6. Maton, K., Dogden, D., Leadbeater, B., Sandler, I., Schellenbach, C., & Solarz, A. (2004). "Strengths-based research and policy: An introduction." *American Psychological Association.* https://doi.org/10.1037/10660-001
7. Buckingham, M. (2007). *Go Put Your Strengths to Work: 6 Powerful Steps to Achieve Outstanding Performance.* Free Press.
8. Cameron, K., Dutton, J., & Quinn, R., I. (2003). *Positive Organizational Scholarship: Foundations of a New Discipline.* Berrett-Koehler.
9. Clifton, D.O., & Harter, J.K. (2003). "Investing in Strengths." In A. K.S. Cameron, B. J.E.
10. Dutton, & C. R.E. Quinn (Eds.), "Positive Organizational Scholarship: Foundations of a New Discipline" (pp. 111-121). San Francisco: Berrett-Koehler Publishers, Inc. https://media.gallup.com/documents/whitepaper--investinginstrengths.pdf
11. Meyers, M., & van Woerkom, M. (2017). "Effects of a Strengths Intervention on General and Work-Related Well-Being: The Mediating Role of Positive Affect." *Journal of Happiness Studies*, 18(3), 671-689. https://doi.org/10.1007/s10902-016-9745-x
12. Woerkom, M., Mostert, K., Els, C., Bakker, A., de Beer, L., & Rothmann, S. (2016). "Strengths use and deficit correction in organizations: Development

and validation of a questionnaire." *European Journal of Work and Organizational Psychology*, 25(6), 960-975.
13. Bushe, G., & Kassam, A. (2005). "When Is Appreciative Inquiry Transformational?: A Meta-Case Analysis." *The Journal of Applied Behavioral Science*, 41(2), 161-181. https://doi.org/10.1177/0021886304270337
14. Cooperrider, D. and Srivastva, S. (1987). "Appreciative inquiry in organizational life." *Organizational Change and Development*, Vol. 1, pp. 129–169.
15. Cooperrider, D. & Whitney, D. (1999). *Appreciative Inquiry: Collaborating for Change*. Berrett-Kohler Publishing
16. Daniels, A. (2016). *Bringing Out the Best in People: How to Apply the Astonishing Power of Positive Reinforcement* (3rd edition). McGraw Hill.
17. Brown, T. (2009). *Change by Design: How Design Thinking Transforms Organizations and Inspires Innovation*. Harper Collings Publishers.
18. Hodges, T., & Clifton, D. (2004). *Strengths-based Development in Practice*. John Wiley & Sons, Inc. https://doi.org/10.1002/9780470939338.ch16
19. Hiemstra, D., & Van Yperen, N. (2015). "The effects of strength-based versus deficit-based self-regulated learning strategies on students' effort intentions." *Motivation and Emotion*, 39(5), 656-668. https://doi.org/10.1007/s11031-015-9488-8
20. Daniels, A. (2016). *Bringing Out the Best in People: How to Apply the Astonishing Power of Positive Reinforcement* (3rd edition). McGraw Hill.
21. Hodges, T., & Clifton, D. (2004). *Strengths-based Development in Practice*. John Wiley & Sons, Inc. https://doi.org/10.1002/9780470939338.ch16
22. Hiemstra, D., & Van Yperen, N. (2015). "The effects of strength-based versus deficit-based self-regulated learning strategies on students' effort intentions." *Motivation and Emotion*, 39(5), 656-668. https://doi.org/10.1007/s11031-015-9488-8
23. Daniels, A., & Daniels, J. (2006). *Performance Management: Changing Behavior That Drives Organizational Effectiveness*. Performance Management Publications.
24. Asplund, J., Lopez, S., Hodges, T., & Harter, J. (2009). "The Clifton StrengthsFinder 2.0 Technical Report: Development and Validation." The Gallup Organization. https://www.researchgate.net/publication/228379158_The_Clifton_StrengthsFinderR_20_Technical_Report_Development_and_Validation
25. Rath, T. (2007). *StrengthsFinder 2.0*. Gallup Press.

Life-Changing Habit #3
Embracing Data-Driven Decisions

"In God we trust, others must have data."

—Ronald D. Snee[1]

OVERVIEW

Technology is collecting a deluge of information that has the potential to make or break any organization. "Analytics-based decision-making is essential for making big decisions and thousands of little ones."[2] Most leaders would agree that growing revenue amid uncertainty amplifies the need for organizations to make data-driven decisions. However, few leaders and organizations effectively use analytics to make better decisions.

To extract value from the vast amount of available information and thrive in the reality of everyday chaos, leaders face two significant challenges. The first challenge involves gathering, processing, and warehousing high-volume, high-speed, and highly diverse data sets. The second challenge is managing the sheer volume of information mined from the data. If not done well, organizations can get buried in the data and miss the opportunity presented.

Data holds a key for helping organizations detect and respond to disruption. Descriptive Data Analytics help make more informed decisions, and Predictive Data Analytics enhance a company's ability to seize new opportunities.

- Descriptive Data Analytics is the interpretation of historical data to better understand changes in a business. Examples include social media usage, organizing survey results, and operational efficiency data trends.
- Predictive Data Analytics is the use of historical data, statistical algorithms, and machine learning to identify the likelihood of future outcomes. Examples include anticipating customer preferences based on past purchasing behaviors, predicting employee retention flight risk based on assessment data, and forecasting workforce staffing levels based on seasonal trends.

Anticipating the unknown creates a competitive advantage when aligned with organizational change capability.[3] A business' ability to be change-resilient and make data-driven decisions is connected to its culture and organizational design.[4] Although not easy to establish, the habit of embracing data-driven decisions creates competitive advantages through better decisions and fostering growth.

Defining Data-Driven Decision-Making

As many leaders and organizations aim to be data-driven, data-driven decision-making has become somewhat of a buzzword. A good working definition for the habit of embracing data-driven decision-making is using facts extracted from data and metrics to guide business decisions that support business goals, rather than relying on experience, intuition, and stories alone.

LIFE-CHANGING HABIT #3: EMBRACING DATA-DRIVEN DECISIONS

VIRTUES OF EMBRACING DATA-DRIVEN DECISIONS

Architecting data-driven culture and designing a data-driven organization are two practical ways (virtues) to embrace data-driven decision-making.

Architecting Data-Driven Cultural Orientation

A company's data-driven decision-making capacity and performance are significantly moderated by culture. "Culture is more powerful than anything else in the organization," and often why good management ideas fail.[5] Focusing only on building analytics capability is ineffective until an organizational culture supports data-driven decision-making.[6] Often, many elements of an organization's culture are not visible daily and drop into the background.

The characteristics of a data-driven cultural orientation include:[7]

- Desiring to find the truth
- Looking for patterns and root causes
- Developing detail-oriented analysis
- Using data to analyze questions
- Appreciating both positive and negative findings in the data
- Making decisions and following through on actions
- Being realistic about when and where to use data analytics

Executive sponsorship is essential, but leaders at all levels in the organization play a vital role in shaping successful organizational culture. Although architecting organizational culture is challenging, making changes often doesn't require considerable investments or physically co-located employees. Leaders can take the following actions to help establish a data-driven cultural orientation.

- Regular attention from leaders is one of the most potent levers leaders have available. Asking employees what data they are using to make decisions is a great start to architecting a data-driven culture.
- Much can be revealed when a business or a leader faces a significant challenge by how they respond. These crucible moments are like a refining fire. It is the heightened emotional intensity that increases individual and organizational learning. When times get tough at work, do leaders ask for data to determine their response, or do the past stories dictate the response?
- Budget allocations reveal the organization's assumptions and beliefs. What receives financial and human resources gets reinforced. Leaders should consider what tools and resources are available to employees who make data-driven decisions.
- The way leaders act and behave outside training events is more significant than what is said or demonstrated within them. Leaders take time to mentor, explain, and show how they routinely use data to make decisions.
- Rewards and recognition come in many different forms, and what is considered a reward varies from person to person. Both what and how rewards are distributed, and what is not rewarded reinforce organizational culture. Rewards and recognition can range from tangible spot compensation bonuses for data-driven decisions to a simple thank-you note when an employee uses data to recognize the desired behaviors.
- Human resource decisions such as hiring, promotions, and terminations can be viewed as a more subtle nuance to culture change because these decisions are influenced by explicitly stated criteria and unstated value priorities. Leaders looking to create a data-driven decision-making cultural orientation will benefit from assessing the skill sets needed within the organization and then hiring, promoting, and exiting targeted employees.

LIFE-CHANGING HABIT #3: EMBRACING DATA-DRIVEN DECISIONS

- Change is essential for organizations to remain competitive and reveals what is vital to employees. When data is used to know what, how, why, and when to implement change, leaders reinforce the importance of data-driven decisions.
- Additional secondary actions to review and consider include organizational design, policies and procedures, rituals and events, workspaces, traditions and stories, and company vision and mission statements.

Organizations are likely to deny the need for culture change. Leaders commonly become anxious at the suggestion of culture change. Overcoming resistance to change begins with establishing a desire for survival and reducing learning anxiety by creating psychological safety. Leaders create psychological safety by proactively helping followers understand and accept the need for a data-driven culture orientation.

Designing a Data-Driven Organization

A well-designed organization works together efficiently and effectively. In a poorly designed organization, there is confusion and waste that inhibits performance.[8] Companies with the right analytics infrastructure and the right talent in the right places have a significant competitive advantage. Talent needs to be structured in alignment with its culture and mission to maximize potential. Companies need to identify the right analytical skills and assess their organizational design to avoid costly mistakes and increase revenue.

Analytical skills include more than the obvious need for technical competence with coding and applications for modeling, forecasting, and statistical analysis. For organizations to be effective with data analytics, they need employees with business process knowledge and skills in negotiating, consulting, communicating, developing others, and quantitative analysis.[9]

Organizations also need analytical leadership at every level, not just in the executive suite. Beyond being good leaders, analytical leaders possess a passion for data analytics, make data-driven decisions, and commit to results. They develop others' analytical capabilities in order to set strategies with analytic performance metrics and seek out and exploit quick wins. They take a long-term view of analytics and grow their analytical networks of people and utilize project portfolios to work across the business and within the limitations of data analytics.[10]

Having the right talent strategy and being clear on the analytical skills your organization needs to compete helps build a successful analytical organization. However, having the right talent with the right skills is not the only challenge. As discussed earlier, having an analytical orientation within an organization's culture is vital to building a successful analytical organization. An organization's perceived value associated with analytics directly influences decisions to align analytical resources across the business.

A critical mass of analytical talent is essential to making better data-driven decisions and determining the optimal organizational design. The challenge is placing the analytical resources close enough to the business to focus on the most critical initiatives while still enabling mutual learning across the analytical resources.

Additionally, design decisions need to consider the organization's analytical culture orientation and the organization's current and desired analytical maturity. The analytical maturity influences the strategic direction, alignment, and commitment needed to achieve the organization's full potential. The following model developed by Davenport, Harris, and Morison identifies five stages of analytical maturity to be considered:

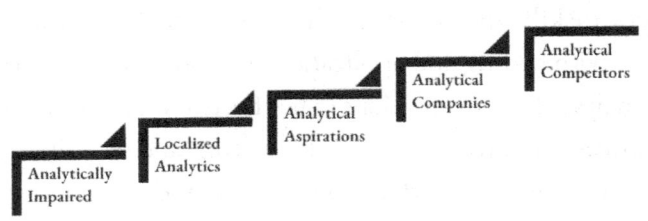

Analytically Impaired → Localized Analytics → Analytical Aspirations → Analytical Companies → Analytical Competitors

Note: Figure adapted from Davenport and Harris (2010) five stages of analytical maturity.[11]

LIFE-CHANGING HABIT #3: EMBRACING DATA-DRIVEN DECISIONS

- Stage 1: Analytically Impaired. There is no companywide visibility or interest in analytics.
- Stage 2: Localized Analytics. There are a few analytical success experiences, but they are isolated across the business.
- Stage 3: Analytical Aspirations. The business is implementing analytical projects to focus on the most strategic applications.
- Stage 4: Analytical Companies. Companywide data-driven decisions are being made.
- Stage 5: Analytical Competitors. The business uses data-driven decisions as a competitive advantage within its industry.

IT JUST FEELS RIGHT

Nora was the CEO of a large retail organization. She had grown up within the organization, holding several highly visible critical roles, and was the first non-family member to hold the chief executive officer position. She also had a role on the company's board of directors and was a strong culture fit with the organization.

Nora's company recently faced significant disruption from emerging new technology that enabled a small competitor to provide customers with better service. Nora, a leader who focused on both results and relationships, was facing her first real crisis as company earnings began to slide. She realized the need to make a decision about retooling operations with the new technology or staying the course with the company's existing technology.

Nora called a meeting with her team of executives with similar deep functional expertise. She asked each leader for their recommendation on retooling operations with the new technology. Each leader shared their insights and stories on how situations like this had been handled in the past. She realized that past decisions were made based on feelings rather than data. Nora was concerned with the lack of quantitative data being used to make a vital company decision. She asked her leaders to go back to their teams and find evidence to support their recommendations.

When Nora reconvened the executive team to hear what they had learned, it became apparent that Nora could not base this decision on data. Her team's data was not considered trustworthy, or the team trusted their insights more than the data. Although the executive team was asking for data, the employees shared that the data itself was not as important as the story about the data.

The culture at Nora's company did not support employees in making data-driven decisions. What was valued was the experience and emotional reaction. As a result, although data were available, the organization was not invested in capturing and cleaning the high-volume retail data.

Nora realized that the company culture was more potent than her CEO role. It is difficult to influence change in an organization with strong traditions. She ultimately decided to introduce the new technology and business processes as an added value for customers versus retooling operations and using only the latest technology. This proved to be a great decision, providing a competitive advantage over the emerging competitor. Earnings were again growing for Nora's company.

EXAMPLES OF LACK OF DATA-DRIVEN DECISION-MAKING

The bad habit of not embracing data-driven decision-making in the workplace can be recognized by the presence of an intuition-oriented culture and experience-structured organizational design.

Intuition-Oriented Culture

Intuition-oriented cultures prefer to rely on advice from employees and experience to make decisions. Intuition or a "gut feeling" is a

LIFE-CHANGING HABIT #3: EMBRACING DATA-DRIVEN DECISIONS

judgment decision that comes to mind for a specific action with a sense of plausibility but without clearly defined reasons or justification.[12] Leaders in these organizations do not place a high value on data. They often lack data analytics infrastructure to support making data-driven decisions.

Two cultural myths are often accepted as facts within an intuition-oriented culture. These myths contribute to a failure to embrace data-driven decision-making.

- Myth #1: Data is unique within a given company
- Myth #2: The application of statistical tools is unique to each company

Most business situations can benefit from data-driven decision-making, although sometimes relying on intuition may make sense. For example, in a crisis when there is no time to gather data systematically or variables cannot be measured. The downside of decisions based only on intuition is the increased risks of bias and blind spots leading to poor decisions compared to data, facts, and analysis.

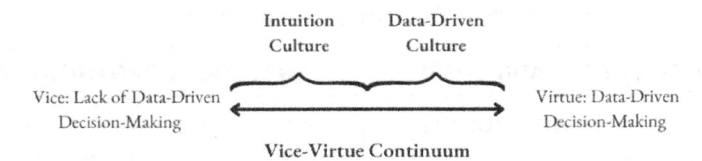

Intuition Culture   Data-Driven Culture

Vice: Lack of Data-Driven Decision-Making ⟵————————⟶ Virtue: Data-Driven Decision-Making

Vice-Virtue Continuum

Example Attributes and Behaviors

INTUITION-ORIENTED	DATA-DRIVEN ORIENTED
• Emphasize experiences within the workplace • Make decisions from what people are saying • Allocate resources based on stories	• Request metrics and reports • Make decisions on patterns and facts from sources of data • Allocate resources based on data and facts

Experience-Structured Organization

Experience-structured organizations usually have more than enough industry-specific knowledge and underestimate the value of organization-wide analytic capability. They lack a clearly articulated strategy for how data analytics supports business outcomes or aligns with business strategies. If analytical capabilities exist they are decentralized, and organizations likely do not have formally defined analytics responsibilities. Data is usually not trusted to be accurate enough to use for making decisions. Advanced tools and resources to extract value from the vast amount of available information are, for the most part, nonexistent. These organizations likely lack processes for gathering and warehousing high-volume, high-speed, and highly diverse data sets. Employees likely feel buried in the data and miss the opportunities presented.

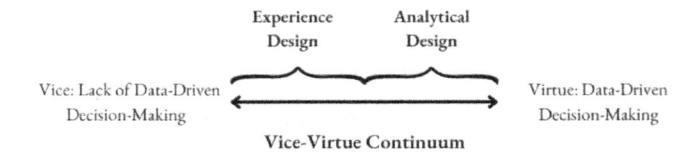

Vice: Lack of Data-Driven Decision-Making ⟵ { Experience Design · Analytical Design } ⟶ Virtue: Data-Driven Decision-Making

Vice-Virtue Continuum

Example Attributes and Behaviors

EXPERIENCE ORGANIZATION	ANALYTICAL ORGANIZATION
• Hire employees with industry experience	• Hire employees with data analytics experience
• Independent functional silos	• Cross-functional teams
• Informal roles with no clear responsibility for data analytics	• Formal analytical roles

LIFE-CHANGING HABIT #3: EMBRACING DATA-DRIVEN DECISIONS

CAUSES, CONSEQUENCES & COMPLICATIONS OF LACK OF DATA-DRIVEN DECISION-MAKING

- Lack of Decision Confidence
- Confusion
- Reduced Productivity
- Lack of Data-Driven Decision-Making (Personal / Professional)
- Inefficient
- Unclear Strategic Foresight
- Lack of Organizational Understanding

Studies have revealed that more than half of Americans routinely use intuition to make significant personal and professional decisions.[13] In some situations, it is impractical for leaders to make data-driven decisions. However, relying on only a feeling of right or wrong would be a big mistake in today's complex and chaotic marketplace. Leaders who effectively harness information gain a competitive advantage.

The causes for the lack of data-driven decision-making can be connected to organizational strategy, culture, organizational design, environment challenges, leadership capability, and motivation. The most significant threats to data-driven decision-making include a lack of executive sponsorship, a clearly articulated strategy, and a culture aligned to data-driven decisions. Strategy drives the organizational structure, and the lack of formal and informal design limits organizational capability. Also, the leader's ego and desire for control may contribute to the lack of data-driven decision-making. A leader's inner need to feel important elevates business decisions to something greater than spreadsheets and facts that others can use to make decisions.[14]

To enable data-driven decision-making, leaders need the technology (to gather, warehouse, and analyze high-volume data), the formal and informal talent (with the capability to analyze data), and the incentives (tied to data-driven decision-making to reinforce its use). It is not easy to manage information and disinformation overload in the deluge of data available. Developing a life-changing habit of embracing data-driven decisions is challenging but essential for leaders and organizations to make better decisions and thrive in the modern workplace.

Decisions make winners and losers in today's competitive workplace. Making data-driven decisions is not the only way leaders can succeed. However, failing to use data analytics creates complications such as:[15]

- Lack of strategic or clear direction during chaotic times
- Confusion about what is and is not working well within the organization
- Failure to leverage technology investments to maximize efficiency and effectiveness
- Increased risk associated with a lack of understanding
- Unclear strategic foresight to see beyond the next crisis

TRANSFORMATIONAL TOOLS & EXERCISES FOR EMBRACING DATA-DRIVEN DECISIONS

How to Assess Culture. Company culture must support business strategies for organizations to be successful. Leaders looking to architect a data-driven decision-making culture should start by clarifying their current business strategies and the characteristics of the existing culture. The Competing Values Framework and the Organizational Culture Assessment Instrument (OCAI) provide organizations with a simple validated method to describe the current and desired company culture.[16]

LIFE-CHANGING HABIT #3: EMBRACING DATA-DRIVEN DECISIONS

The Competing Values Framework identifies four fundamentally different cultures:

1. *Clan Culture* creates a collaborative atmosphere similar to a family. The role of leadership is as a facilitator, mentor, and team builder. This culture emphasizes the value of teamwork, participation, and a consensus decision-making style, leading to more intuitive decisions. This culture creates value through individual commitment, communication effectiveness, and development.
2. *Adhocracy Culture* creates an energetic and entrepreneurial atmosphere. The role of leadership is as an innovator, entrepreneur, and visionary. This culture stresses the importance of research and continuous improvement. This culture creates value through innovative ideas, transformation over transaction, and nimbleness.
3. *Market Culture* creates a competitive, fast-paced, results-oriented environment. The role of leadership is as challenger, competitor, and achiever. This culture highlights coming in first, leading to a more data-driven decision-making orientation, as external data analysis can create a competitive advantage. This culture creates value through capturing market share, meeting or exceeding goals, and profitability.
4. *Hierarchy Culture* is a top-down, formal rule-based atmosphere. The role of leadership is as management, supervision, and organization. This culture emphasizes efficient, reliable, and cost-effective performance, leading to a more data-driven decision-making orientation as internal data analysis can create improved efficiency and reliability. This culture creates value through promptness, consistency, control, and certainty.

For more information regarding the OCAI, please go to www.ocai-online.com.

How to Improve Your Analytic Organization Design. The following is a simple organizational assessment used to enhance talent management, development, and recruiting strategies to support data-driven decision-making. The evaluation involves counting the number of formal and informal human analytical resources across the organization and assessing their depth of analytical capability within three categories of analytical tasks:[17]

- Level 1: capable of workbench, standard reports, and alerts
- Level 2: capable of multidimensional analysis, analytical applications, and data visualization
- Level 3: capable of what-if planning, predictive modeling, and statistical analysis

Table 1
Analytical skill organizational assessment example

ORGANIZATIONAL FUNCTION	ANALYTICAL RESOURCES	LEVEL 1	LEVEL 2	LEVEL 3
Operations	25	Advanced	Intermediate	Foundational
Marketing	5	Foundational	Intermediate	Expert
Human Resources	5	Foundational	Basic	Basic

Note: This table is an example used to demonstrate a hypothetical organizational, analytical skills assessment adapted from Davenport et al. (2010).

Using this assessment will help you:

- Validate the existing formal and informal analytical organization structure.
- Identify opportunities to improve the current formal and informal analytical structure to align with the strategy.
- Evaluate structural options and identify areas that need to be optimized.

LIFE-CHANGING HABIT #3: EMBRACING DATA-DRIVEN DECISIONS

- Create a detailed organizational structure to align with the strategy and facilitate the implementation.
- Visualize the organization's analytical talent structure and capability to easily identify organizational design talent strengths and opportunities.

KEY POINTS—EMBRACING DATA-DRIVEN DECISIONS

- Technology allows companies to collect a deluge of information that has the potential to make or break any organization.
- Making data-driven decisions is not the only way leaders can succeed. However, failing to use data analytics creates complications.
- Data holds a key for helping organizations detect and respond to disruption.
- Data-driven decision-making uses facts extracted from data and metrics to guide business decisions that support business goals, rather than relying on experience, intuition, and stories alone.
- An organization's ability to improve its change resilience and data-driven decision-making are connected to its company culture and organizational design.
- Focusing only on building analytics capability is ineffective until an organizational culture supports data-driven decision-making.
- Executive sponsorship is essential, but leaders at all levels in the organization play a vital role in shaping organizational culture in business.
- Leaders should exercise caution and approach culture change thoughtfully or risk being seen as a problem.
- Companies with the proper analytics infrastructure and the right talent in the right places have a significant competitive advantage.
- The organizational design challenge is placing the analytical resources close enough to the business to focus on the most critical initiatives while still enabling mutual learning across the analytical resources.

REFLECTION QUESTIONS—EMBRACING DATA-DRIVEN DECISIONS

- Do you talk with others about what data is essential to consider when making decisions?
- When a crisis arises, how do you respond? Do you ask for data to help make decisions?
- What data is vital to making better decisions?
- What data do you trust and pay attention to regularly? How could you extract value from available data?

• • •

Endnotes

1. Snee, R. D. (1988). "Mathematics Is Only One Tool That Statisticians Use." *The College Mathematics Journal, 19*(1), 30. https://doi.org/10.2307/2686698
2. Bartlett, R. (2013). *A Practitioner's Guide to Data Analytics: Using Data Analysis to Improve Your Organization's Decision Making and Strategy.* McGraw Hill.
3. van Rijmenam, M., Erekhinskaya, T., Schweitzer, J., & Williams, M. (2019). "Avoid being the Turkey: How big data analytics changes the game of strategy in times of ambiguity and uncertainty." *Long Range Planning, 52*(5), 101841. doi:10.1016/j.lrp.2018.05.007
4. Upadhyay, P., & Kumar, A. (2020). "The intermediating role of organizational culture and internal analytical knowledge between the capability of big data analytics and a firm's performance." *International Journal of Information Management,* 52, 102100. doi:10.1016/j.ijinfomgt.2020.102100
5. Schneider, W. (2000). "Why good management ideas fail." *Strategy & Leadership,* 28(1), 24-29. doi:10.1108/10878570010336001
6. Upadhyay, P., & Kumar, A. (2020). "The intermediating role of organizational culture and internal analytical knowledge between the capability of big data analytics and a firm's performance." *International Journal of Information Management,* 52, 102100. https://doi.org/10.1016/j.ijinfomgt.2020.102100

7. Davenport, T., Harris, J., & Morison, R. (2010). *Analytics at Work: Smarter Decisions, Better Results.* Harvard Business Review Press. MA.
8. Burton, R., Obel, B., & Håkonsson, D. (2020). *Organizational Design: A Step-By-Step Approach* (Fourth ed.). Cambridge University Press.
9. Bartlett, R. (2013). *A Practitioner's Guide to Data Analytics: Using Data Analysis to Improve Your Organization's Decision Making and Strategy.* McGraw Hill.
10. Davenport, T., Harris, J., & Morison, R. (2010). *Analytics at Work: Smarter Decisions, Better Results.* Harvard Business Press. MA.
11. ibid.
12. Hodgkinson, G., Sadler-Smith, E., Burke, L., Claxton, G., & Sparrow, P. (2009). "Intuition in Organizations: Implications for Strategic Management." *Long Range Planning,* 42(3), 277-297. https://doi.org/10.1016/j.lrp.2009.05.003
13. Garrett, R., & Weeks, B. (2017). "Epistemic beliefs' role in promoting misperceptions and conspiracist ideation." *PLOS ONE,* 12(9), e0184733-e0184733. https://doi.org/10.1371/journal.pone.0184733
14. Bonabeau, E. (2003). "Don't trust your gut." *Harvard Business Review,* 81(5), 116-130.
15. Davenport, T., Harris, J. G., & Morison, R. (2010). *Analytics at Work: Smarter Decisions, Better Results.* Harvard Business Press. MA.
16. Cameron, K., Quinn, R., Degraff, J., & Thakor, A. (2006). *Competing Values Leadership: Creating Value in Organizations.* E. Elgar Pub. https://doi.org/10.4337/9781847201560
17. Davenport, T., Harris, J., & Morison, R. (2010). *Analytics at Work: Smarter Decisions, Better Results.* Harvard Business Press. MA.

Life-Changing Habit #4
Maximizing Purpose

"Working hard for something we don't care about is called stress; working hard for something we love is called passion."
—SIMON SINEK[1]

OVERVIEW

Why am I here? Why am I a leader? Work and career without purpose are never genuinely satisfying, even though they can be financially rewarding. The most significant opportunities to transform our lives, the lives of those we lead, the organizations we belong to, and the communities where we live, are within our purpose.[2] Maximizing your purpose creates passion. Purpose channels passion in directions that make a difference, like a rudder on a ship. Knowing and living within your purpose unlocks success and significance for you as a leader and for your team.

The link between trust and purpose is of great importance to leadership. At its essence, leadership is a relationship, and trust is foundational to the most valuable relationships. Now more than ever, followers are looking to know that leaders believe in something in addition to the bottom line. They don't want talking heads that repeat a company mantra. They want leaders that will stand up for and do what is right.

In his poem, "The Voiceless," Oliver Wendell Holmes concluded that many of us will go to our graves with our music still inside and unplayed.[3] Sadly, many leaders may spend more time thinking about what they will wear to work than the purpose of their work. As a result, they may be dressed for success yet fail to achieve personal and professional significance. Some leaders become anxious with introspection. Finding an individual leadership purpose can be challenging in a world full of powerful and influential personal and professional advice about leadership. It is easy for leaders to become a prisoner to a general leadership identity defined by others.

The habit of maximizing purpose makes a difference not only by enabling you to say no, but also when to say yes. In today's fast-paced and turbulent digital marketplace, the decisive direction that purpose creates is a competitive advantage for individuals and organizations. Purpose leads to personal engagement, which energizes the leader and their team amid complexity and volatility. Working for something bigger than yourself increases your motivation and courage to pursue more significant challenges. Purpose helps stretch you to move outside of comfort. This is where the most extraordinary transformation occurs.

Defining Purpose

Goals, meaning, and purpose are sometimes used interchangeably as definitions. It is helpful to understand their similarities and differences so that the description of purpose is clear. Goals are what we try to achieve and help sustain momentum in life and work. Meaning is the value we ascribe to something. According to Holocaust survivor and psychiatrist Victor Frankl, "meaning is the primary force in life," and achieving meaning creates significance.[4] As a leader, purpose is the intention to achieve something personally meaningful through shared goals

LIFE-CHANGING HABIT #4: MAXIMIZING PURPOSE

for the collective benefit between the leader, individual employees, the team, the organization, and the world. As an organization, purpose is the intention to achieve something that is organizationally meaningful through organizational goals for the collective benefit of the organization and the communities in which they operate.

VIRTUES OF MAXIMIZING PURPOSE

Three practical ways (virtues) to maximize your purpose are knowing yourself, focusing on executing what is important, and delegating effectively.

Knowing Yourself

When you know yourself, you have the insight to recognize bad leadership habits and lead with life-changing habits. We all see the world from our unique point of view. We tell ourselves stories about our strengths and areas where we need to be better, as well as what is or is not good leadership. Our patterns of behavior are shaped by past experiences and the words used to describe our actions. With good intentions, we set out to lead as best we can. Then life happens, and we realize we have blind spots and distortions that can jeopardize our goals.

According to Socrates, "to know thyself is the beginning of wisdom."[5] Consider the passenger-side rearview mirror on a car. The required safety warning on the mirror states that objects are closer than they appear. Also, in driver's education we learn the mirror has blind spots. These distortions and blind spots can be hazardous for a driver if what is seen and not seen is not interpreted within the proper context.

To know yourself means that you can see yourself objectively, you are aware of similarities and differences from others, and you understand the perspective from which you see others and the world. The researched benefits of knowing yourself are numerous, including improved relationships,[6] self-control, decision-making, and ultimately life satisfaction.[7] Leaders can make bad decisions without understanding the wisdom of knowing their distortions and blind spots.

The higher you move within any organization, the less objective you are and the less general feedback you tend to receive. Knowing yourself personally and professionally becomes more critical. The last thing an executive needs in today's demanding workplace is someone or something telling them what they already know. The better the quality of the feedback you receive, the better the decisions you can make. Executive coaching combined with executive assessments helps reveal deep insights into areas which, with attention, lead to enhanced potential. Research supports that a coach's timely and appropriate use of executive assessment leads to improved personal awareness and organizational outcomes.[8] While no one categorization system exists for executive assessments, these are the ways I have found it helpful to consider the various types of assessments and their particular value for knowing yourself.[9]

- **360 evaluation:** This type of multi-rater instrument is a proven tool to collect feedback from multiple directions relative to the executive's position within an organization and an executive's leadership performance, skills, and contributions. Leadership is a relationship, and it is vital to know what others think. When we consider only ourselves, we have an incomplete understanding. While 360-degree feedback effectively improves leadership skills across all cultures, it is most effective in cultures with low power distance and individualistic values such as Germany, the Netherlands, the United Kingdom, and the United States.

- **Diagnostic:** This type of evaluation typically has a lesser degree of reliability, validity, or fairness and does not require specialized training to interpret. It may or may not provide norm comparisons versus self-reporting. Typically, you need only to read a book or white paper to make sense of the evaluation.

- **Assessment:** This type of evaluation provides normed feedback and may or may not be validated. Typically, assessments require some formal training to interpret.
- **Test:** This type of evaluation is scientifically proven to meet reliability, validity, and fairness standards. These assessments require advanced education in clinical or industrial and organizational psychology to interpret.

In today's increasingly complex and culturally diverse workplace, leaders who can accurately perceive, assess, and regulate their own and others' emotions can better promote unity and team morale.[10] Studies have demonstrated that followers perceive leaders with a heightened emotional intelligence as being successful and effective. Increased awareness may enable leaders to create shared emotional experiences that enhance personal and follower growth and well-being. Leaders are better prepared to adapt appropriately in a given situation when they possess a heightened self-awareness.

Focused on Executing What Is Important

Being able to bridge the gap between good intentions and results is increasingly essential and enables leaders to maximize their purpose. It is easy to lose focus on executing what is necessary when a typical day is filled with a constant barrage of texts, emails, and back-to-back meetings. The typical workday pulls the leader toward what is urgent at the moment versus what is essential to purpose. Additionally, research has found that we all tend to focus on tasks with short completion requirements. Important tasks that are often more rewarding and complex get pushed aside for quick wins.[11] Leaders who maximize purpose prioritize working on the important over urgent, spend most of their time working where they have influence, and efficiently achieve meaningful results. Delegating is key. Impact where you can, but also allow your followers to make an impact where they can.

What is urgent is not always important. Urgent things are those unplanned or delayed events in a day that demand the leader's immediate attention. Important events are planned events with significant implications for personal, professional, or organizational goals. Making choices to focus on what is important frees up time and energy so you can focus on your purpose.

> "Everything requires time. It is the one truly universal condition. All work takes place in time and uses up time."
> —PETER DRUCKER[12]

You cannot influence everything that concerns you. For example, you can be worried about how a competitor is marketing their products; however, you have no direct impact. Focusing on issues within your ability to influence increases your impact on purpose. Concentrating on areas of concern without influence wastes time and energy.[13]

Meetings are costly. Leaders spend much of their time at work in meetings. Effective meeting skills moderate your ability to maximize purpose. Unfortunately, most meetings become a waste of time. With an increased reliance on virtual meetings, this sad perception about meetings has increased. However, research has identified that the use of an agenda, keeping minutes, being punctual, the meeting environment, and having a designated meeting leader are factors that make for good meetings. The purpose of the meeting should be clear and concise, and it also will help clarify exactly who is required to be in the meeting.

Running a virtual meeting is not simply using the most sophisticated or newest platform. Deciding when and how to meet virtually are essential considerations for leaders to engage efficiently and effectively in an increasingly virtual workforce. Determining why to meet informs the best virtual method and the meeting needed capabilities (e.g., hearing, discerning visual cues, and experiencing what attendees are seeing) for virtual meetings. Additionally, the number of meeting participants and the meeting duration influence the best virtual method and needed capabilities. Virtual meetings tend to become less effective with more significant numbers of participants and longer durations.[14] A clear meeting purpose is always helpful. Time is precious; use it wisely.

Effective Delegation

One of the more difficult shifts a leader makes is growing from doing to leading. At times effective leading involves successful delegation. Although many leaders are overworked and recognize the need to empower and develop employees, many are reluctant to do so. Giving up authority and responsibility can seem counterintuitive. Leaders who maximize their purpose tend to approach delegating with intent and a win-win mindset for the leader and the follower.

Effective delegation improves job satisfaction, responsibility, performance, intrinsic motivation,[15] confidence, and career development.[16] Delegation signals trust and support from the leader to followers, resulting in increased follower effort and performance. Additionally, effective delegation improves followers' perceptions of the leader's performance.[17]

Effective delegation involves carefully considering the task, situation, employee capacity and capability, communication, and leadership support and reinforcement to create success. Delegation increases work-related discretion and the authority to make decisions without consulting the leader for pre-approval. Effective delegation is dynamic and involves the transfer of responsibility and authority from the leader to a willing follower. Effective delegation is not assigning a task or decision to an unwilling delegate. Giving the delegate the responsibility without the authority does not work. Not having the authority to act results in wasted time and frustration for both you and the delegate, not to mention whether the job gets done or not.

Culture and the quality of the leader-follower relationship moderate the effectiveness of delegating. High-power distance cultures such as in China or Japan limit the positive effects of delegation on performance.[18] Additionally, the presence of high levels of trust in high-quality leader-follower relationships enhance positive outcomes of delegating.

CHASING SUCCESS

David was a small-business entrepreneur within a large organization. One night, while out for dinner with his brother, the two hatched an idea on the back of the restaurant napkin to create an innovative consumer products company.

David and his brother Jim had lived together in a two-bedroom apartment since graduating from college. Financially, they were barely able to pay their bills. Nothing glamorous about it. This new business represented a shared goal with the potential to achieve financial success and make a difference in the marketplace.

They quit their jobs and started the new company, working long hours every day of the week. Both the company and the brothers' relationship were at risk of failing. The company's sales were mainly to friends and family. Then, as years went by, the small business started to grow. However, the long hours didn't provide the financial return they had envisioned. Jim and David became increasingly frustrated. They would frequently have sessions that seemed more like street fights than problem-solving.

LIFE-CHANGING HABIT #4: MAXIMIZING PURPOSE

Jim was the first to realize that if they continued this way, with long hours and growing tension, it would lead to company failure. Jim decided to get a place of his own and leave their shared apartment. Although this would increase their expenses, making the financial situation more difficult, he felt it best for the company and the relationship. David was disappointed and began to question if he should sell his part of the company and go back to his old job.

The move was completed as planned. The brothers fought less, and the company continued to grow. Jim and David began enjoying financial success from their many years of hard work. Customers would frequently stop them around town and tell them how much they appreciated the story of how two brothers took an idea from a napkin to a multimillion-dollar company.

Unfortunately, the distance did not help Jim and David's relationship. They grew further apart, and the good ole days of the shared apartment were a distant memory. At this time, in reflection, David and Jim realized that their laser focus on company goals and their financial success came with a hidden personal cost to their relationship.

Without understanding your purpose and focusing on individual goals, you can achieve success and miss out on what is meaningful in life. Maximizing purpose cannot be achieved without careful consideration of what is most meaningful to you, your team, and the world.

EXAMPLES OF UNINTENTIONAL LEADERSHIP

The bad habit of unintentional leadership can be recognized by a lack of self-awareness, ineffective delegation, and a pattern of focusing on executing what seems urgent.

Lack of Self-Awareness

Lacking self-awareness limits your ability to realize your professional and personal goals. It's like trying to navigate a ship without a sextant. Leaders who lack self-awareness are naive about their habits and can easily develop bad habits. A sense of your career stalling, lacking direction, or a lack of excitement from learning something new are potential signs of a lack of self-awareness.

Overestimating your ability can lead to negative consequences for your performance and the organization.[19] Often, leaders who have a distorted view of their strengths and weaknesses cannot effectively regulate their emotions and behaviors. The symptoms of a lack of self-awareness include negative consequences to your physical health, work performance, and social interactions.[20]

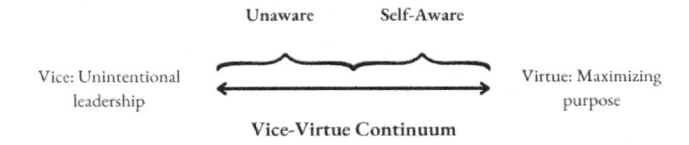

```
                    Unaware      Self-Aware
Vice: Unintentional   ⏜             ⏜         Virtue: Maximizing
    leadership    ←─────────────────────→         purpose
                      Vice-Virtue Continuum
```

Example Attributes and Behaviors

UNAWARE	SELF-AWARE
• Lack of self-control • Distant from others • Self-absorbed • Lack of confidence	• Self-regulated behaviors and emotional responses • High-quality relationships • Empathic • Competent and confident

Focused on Executing What Is Urgent

If you can't recognize when you are overly focused on the urgent, then everything is important, so nothing is important. When leaders lack an

LIFE-CHANGING HABIT #4: MAXIMIZING PURPOSE

understanding of their purpose, they can't clearly identify what is truly important from what is not. Executive leaders need clarity of purpose to cut through the noise of the day. Without clarity of purpose to focus on what is important, leaders waste effort and time—both of which are scarce commodities at the executive level of any organization.

Leaders in this situation often feel trapped in a constant state of meeting overload. Without a clear understanding of what is important, the leader's performance, job satisfaction, and results are negatively impacted. This lack of clarity on what is truly important results in a form of attention deficit disorder as leaders feel trapped in a sea of important challenges.[21] Followers become confused, and the leader's lack of clarity puts their followers' personal and professional goals at risk.

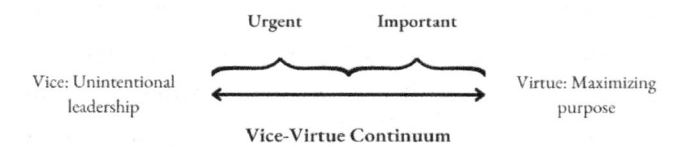

Vice: Unintentional leadership ←——— Urgent | Important ———→ Virtue: Maximizing purpose

Vice-Virtue Continuum

Example Attributes and Behaviors

URGENT	IMPORTANT
• Has a hard time saying no • Everything looks important • Unaware of their purpose • Spend time on areas of concern	• Able to clearly identify what is important • Says no to the urgent and unimportant work • Able to articulate and act upon their purpose • Spend time on areas of influence

Ineffective Delegation

When leaders are caught between the pressure of urgent and important work demands, delegating often becomes an underutilized leadership approach. Yet year after year, one of the top five reasons high-potential employees leave their current employer is for an exciting new career development opportunity. Employees are looking for opportunities to take on assignments to learn and grow. Effective delegation may be the very thing executive leaders need to master now more than ever to win in the marketplace. According to leadership expert John Maxwell, "If you want to do a few small things right, do them yourself. If you want to do great things and make an impact, learn to delegate."[22]

One of the most ineffective delegation habits is working from the point of view that if you want to get something done, you must do it yourself. This approach causes leaders to hold on to work rather than looking for win-win delegating opportunities within their team. Ineffective delegation wastes time and resources, lowers team morale, and increases frustration and confusion. Another common delegation failure is assigning a task or decision to an unwilling employee or giving responsibility without the authority to do the work. Neither of these approaches is effective. Having the responsibility but lacking the authority results in wasted time and frustration for both the leader and the delegate. Unfortunately, some leaders over delegate tasks and decisions to their high performers under the guise of development. But when a leader assigns work to an unwilling delegate, it leads to frustration and job dissatisfaction. While the leader intended to advance and retain their top talent, they risk losing their best and potentially punishing the very performance they want.

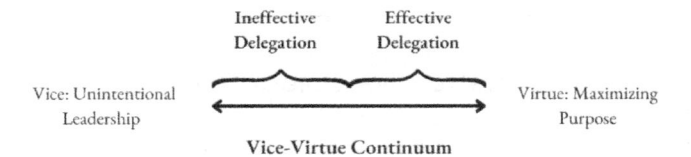

	Ineffective Delegation	Effective Delegation	
Vice: Unintentional Leadership	←————————→		Virtue: Maximizing Purpose

Vice-Virtue Continuum

Example Attributes and Behaviors

INEFFECTIVE DELEGATION	EFFECTIVE DELEGATION
• Under and over delegating • Failing to communicate • Delegating and walking away	• Careful consideration of the task, situation, employee capacity, and capability • Communicating effectively with delegate and stakeholders • Providing support and reinforcement

CAUSES, CONSEQUENCES & COMPLICATIONS OF UNINTENTIONAL LEADERSHIP

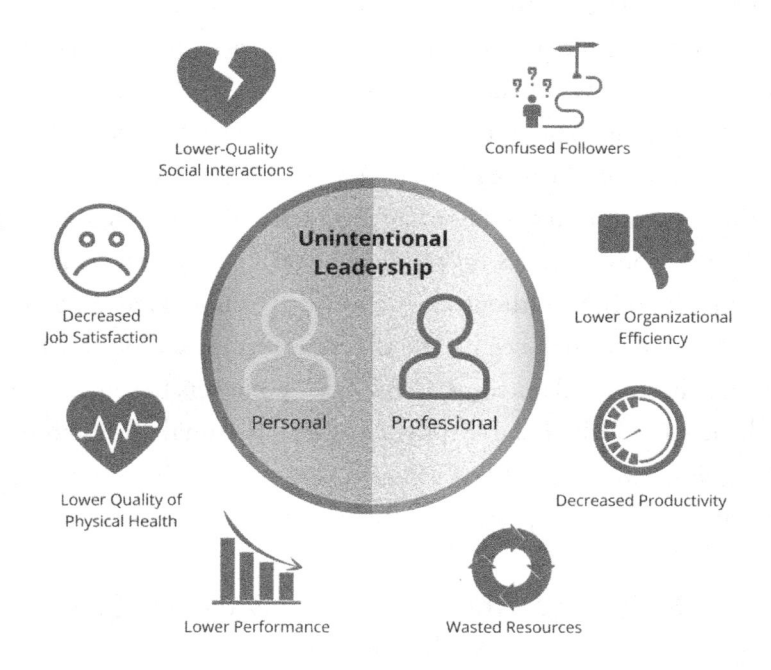

Lower-Quality Social Interactions

Confused Followers

Decreased Job Satisfaction

Unintentional Leadership

Personal | Professional

Lower Organizational Efficiency

Lower Quality of Physical Health

Decreased Productivity

Lower Performance

Wasted Resources

Many potential causes contribute to the bad habit of unintentional leadership. In modern organizations, it's easy to get caught up in the trap of being focused on what is urgent. Unfortunately, an executive leader's world tends to reward "firefighting." Leaders find themselves running from meeting to meeting and being rewarded for fixing urgent problems. Focusing on better self-awareness, delegating effectively, and focusing on what is important to maximize your leadership purpose gets pushed and pulled aside to make room for completing daily tasks. This fast-paced environment makes it easy to fall into the trap of confusing the urgent with the important, creating an illusion of maximizing purpose. The higher you move up in an organization, the more critical it becomes to have clarity of purpose to cut through the noise and maximize your leadership purpose.

Narcissism refers to a highly self-involved personality. Narcissists generally lack self-awareness, and their egos tend to reject any potential negative blind spots in themselves. Research has demonstrated that narcissistic employees are likely to emerge as leaders in groups that lack familiarity with one another. Leaders with narcissistic tendencies struggle with maximizing purpose because they tend to exclude consideration of others and causes beyond themselves.

Complications arising from unintentional leadership ultimately limit the success and significance of the leader, their team, and their organization. Success and significance are not accidents. A lack of self-awareness has negative consequences on physical health, work performance, and social interactions.[23] Without a clear and shared understanding of what is important, meetings negatively affect performance, job satisfaction, meeting behavior, and outcomes achieved.[24] Followers become confused, and the leader's lack of clarity puts followers' personal and professional goals at risk. Every leader has the same amount of time in a day, and unintentional leadership wastes time and resources.

TRANSFORMATIONAL TOOLS & EXERCISES FOR MAXIMIZING PURPOSE

Keys to 360-Degree Assessments. 360-Degree assessments can be a valuable tool for helping you reveal hidden strengths and blind spots. The following are six keys to 360-degree assessment success:[25]

LIFE-CHANGING HABIT #4: MAXIMIZING PURPOSE

1. Maximize value by linking behaviors assessed to organizational values and leadership style (keep it short and simple).
2. Promote valid feedback by thoughtful consideration of raters with leader input.
3. Educate raters on the assessment and its purpose ahead of administering.
4. Predict how raters will respond before receiving the actual survey feedback.
5. Utilize a coach for debriefing the feedback, delineating SMART goals, and serving as an accountability partner.
6. Utilize 360-degree assessment as part of an organization-wide initiative.

How to Improve Self-Regulation. Research suggests that you can change your self-reported personality traits by changing daily patterns of thoughts, feelings, and behaviors. In other words, if your ability to self-regulate is strong enough, you can always do the right thing in a given situation and not just what your inclinations or past experiences would suggest. Working on improving self-regulation in one part of your life can improve your ability to regulate another. For example, committing to a physical exercise program is linked to improvements in self-regulation in areas beyond exercise.[26]

Additionally, self-awareness and self-regulation can be improved with mindfulness[27] training such as breathing and meditation exercises. If you are looking to improve your self-regulation capability, you can use the Short Self-Regulation Questionnaire (SSRQ) to measure pre- and post-intervention. The process used with the SSRQ consists of the following seven steps:[28]

1. Getting relevant information on your behavior
2. Evaluating the information and comparing it to the standard
3. Considering making a change

4. Looking for alternatives
5. Devising a plan
6. Implementing and maintaining the plan
7. Assessing the effectiveness of your plan

How to Find Your Purpose. One way to find your purpose is to consider the following equation created by Richard Leider:[29]

Gifts + Passions + Values = Purpose

- Step 1: Identify your gifts. Everyone has gifts. What do you best that you enjoy most?
- Step 2: Identify your passions. Where do you apply your gifts? What is worth doing?
- Step 3: Identify your values. What do you stand for?

After answering these questions, discuss them with your community and family to see if they agree and have other insights. For example, my purpose is to lead others toward greater understanding and simple solutions that avoid costly mistakes to achieve complex personal and professional challenges.

For more information regarding this purpose equation, read *The Power of Purpose* by Richard Leider.

How to Effectively Manage Urgent vs. Important: It is easy to get trapped focusing on what is urgent, thus sacrificing what is important. To manage time effectively and efficiently, it is helpful to consider spending time on tasks based on their urgency and importance. The following time management matrix was popularized by Stephen Covey in his book *The 7 Habits of Highly Effective People*:[30]

LIFE-CHANGING HABIT #4: MAXIMIZING PURPOSE

Time Management Matrix:

QUADRANT 1: IMPORTANT AND URGENT	QUADRANT 2: IMPORTANT AND NOT URGENT
QUADRANT 3: NOT IMPORTANT BUT URGENT	QUADRANT 4: NOT IMPORTANT AND NOT URGENT

To use this matrix, review your calendar and list the tasks and activities you need to accomplish within your workday. Next, think of each activity, place them in one of the four quadrants, and allocate your time to those with the highest priority. Quadrant two is where you maximize purpose and spend time achieving your personal and professional goals. If you spend a lot of your day in quadrant one, consider opportunities to improve project management and schedule tasks ahead of time to avoid urgency. Quadrant three activities can be great activities to consider for delegating, and quadrant four activities should be avoided.

How to Maximize Team Meeting Effectiveness. Meetings don't have to be ineffective. The following ideas are taken from Patrick Lencioni in his book *Death by Meeting*, and lean process improvement methodology can help leaders improve team meeting effectiveness and efficiency:

- Scrum Meetings: The purpose of these meetings is to connect on schedules and keep everyone informed of activities. The suggested frequency is daily for less than 15 minutes. Topics include what you did yesterday, what you will do today, and any things getting in the way. The leader's responsibility is to resolve these issues as quickly as possible.
- Tactical Meetings: These meetings are scheduled weekly to resolve identified issues at a team level. These meetings should last less than 90 minutes, and the agenda is driven by a review of topics connected to goals.

- Strategic Meetings: The purpose of these meetings is to discuss critical issues impacting long-term goal success. The suggested frequency is monthly for less than four hours.
- Review Meetings: These meetings are scheduled quarterly off-site to review competition, industry trends, and talent development. These meetings should be agenda-driven and last less than two days.

Additionally, the following meeting agenda template can help participants prepare in advance and focus meetings on what is most important. Each section of the template should be filled out in advance—except for the outcomes and decisions section used to keep minutes during the meeting. A good practice is to leave time at the end of each meeting to review the outcomes and decisions made to ensure alignment and clarify the next actions.

MEETING TOPIC		
Date:	Time:	Location:
Meeting Objectives:		
Agenda Items:		Outcomes and Decisions
Company Values		

How to Improve Virtual Meeting Effectiveness. Meeting objectives, size, and length have significant moderating effects on method effectiveness. The following table adapted from Standaert, Viereck, and Cox provides a guide for selecting the most effective virtual meeting method at the lowest cost.[31]

LIFE-CHANGING HABIT #4: MAXIMIZING PURPOSE

MEETING OBJECTIVE	MEETING PARTICIPANTS		MEETING LENGTH	
	<5	>5	<1 HR	>1 HR
Exchanging Information	Audio	Video	Audio	Video
Making Decisions	Video	Video		Video
Communicating Sentiments	Video	Telepresence	Video	Telepresence
Building Relationships	Telepresence	Face-to-Face	Telepresence	Face-to-Face

Effective Delegation: Effective delegation can be challenging. Spending a little time and effort upfront to consider the task, situation, employee, communication, and leadership support is crucial to delegate effectively. Use the following five-step checklist to improve your delegating skills.

- **Step 1.** Decide if you should delegate. Delegating during crises with critical benefits or harm to the organization is not appropriate. Determine if delegating will help you use your time better or potentially develop others for succession or similar future work. Circumstances with tight timelines with severe or long-term consequences do not allow for mistakes or coaching for development.
- **Step 2.** Decide to whom you will delegate the decision or task. Consider if they have the experience, knowledge, skills, tools, resources, and willingness needed to succeed. Delegating to an employee who is overloaded can lead to costly mistakes. When using delegation for development, consider how to best support the delegate's development. Delegating to a follower who needs your direction to complete the task is a mistake. Doing a task for the first time and not knowing how you are doing is frustrating.

- **Step 3**. Communicate what you are delegating, timelines, outcome expectations, and why you are delegating. Write it down and discuss it with the delegate to make sure they accept. Clarify if you will keep some of the elements of the task or decision yourself and the desired outcomes. Explain the reasons for why you are delegating and why you chose them. Discuss the tools and resources available and, as appropriate, development coaching.
- **Step 4**. Communicate with others. Decide what critical relationships are involved in this work and make sure they know what and to whom you have delegated the task or decision.
- **Step 5**. Provide feedback, incentives, and consequences. Monitor performance and provide corrective and appreciative feedback along the way so the delegate knows how they are doing. After completing the task of making the decision, evaluate the delegate's performance and let them know how they did.

KEY POINTS—MAXIMIZING PURPOSE

- Work and a career without purpose are never truly satisfying, even though they can be financially rewarding.
- Purpose leads to personal engagement, which energizes the leader and their team amid complexity and volatility.
- Finding your specific leadership purpose can be challenging in a world full of powerful personal and professional advice about leadership.
- As a leader, your purpose is to achieve something personally meaningful through shared goals for the collective benefit between the leader, the employee, the team, the organization, and the world.
- When you know yourself, you have the insight to recognize bad leadership habits and lead with life-changing habits.

LIFE-CHANGING HABIT #4: MAXIMIZING PURPOSE

- Leaders who maximize purpose prioritize working on the important over urgent, spend most of their time working where they have influence, and efficiently achieve meaningful results.
- Executive leaders who maximize their purpose tend to approach delegating with intention and a win-win mindset.
- Effective delegation improves job satisfaction, responsibility, performance, intrinsic motivation, confidence, and career development.
- High levels of trust in high-quality leader-follower relationships enhance the positive outcomes of delegating.

REFLECTION QUESTIONS—MAXIMIZING PURPOSE

- What is your happiest memory?
- What makes you lose track of time?
- How do you define success and significance?
- What is one problem you see in the world that is worth your sacrifice?
- Answer the following question for yourself, then ask your team and your community. It is five years from today, and everything you or they had hoped and dreamed about has come true. Describe what you or they see: What are you or they doing differently? What are others doing differently?
- Who are the high-potential employees on your team, and what development do they need?
- What are your leadership blind spots and hidden strengths?
- Are you delegating effectively, i.e., considering the task, situation, employee capacity and capability, communication, and the leadership support and reinforcement to create success?

• • •

Endnotes

1. Sinek, S. (@simonsinek). "Working hard for something we don't care about is called stress; working hard for something we love is called passion." Twitter, February 28, 2012. https://twitter.com/simonsinek/status/174469085726375936
2. Hollensbe, E., Wookey, C., Hickey, L., & George, G. (2014). "Organizations with purpose." *Academy of Management Journal*, 57(5), 1227-1234. https://doi.org/10.5465/amj.2014.4005
3. Holmes, O.W. (1889). *The Autocrat of the Breakfast-Table: Every Man His Own Boswell*. W.Scott; W.J. Gage.
4. Frankl, V.E. (1959). *Man's Search for Meaning: An Introduction to Logotherapy*. Boston: Beacon. (p.121).
5. Brickhouse, Thomas C.; Smith, Nicholas D. (1994). *Plato's Socrates*. Oxford University Press.
6. Oltmanns, T., Gleason, M., Klonsky, E., & Turkheimer, E. (2005). "Meta-perception for pathological personality traits: Do we know when others think that we are difficult?" *Consciousness and Cognition*, 14(4), 739-751. https://doi.org/10.1016/j.concog.2005.07.001
7. Wilson, T., & Gilbert, D. (2005). "Affective Forecasting: Knowing What to Want." *Current Directions in Psychological Science: A Journal of the American Psychological Society*, 14(3), 131-134. https://doi.org/10.1111/j.0963-7214.2005.00355.x
8. Athanasopoulou, A., & Dopson, S. (2018). "A systematic review of executive coaching outcomes: Is it the journey or the destination that matters the most?" *The Leadership Quarterly*, 29(1), 70-88.
9. Goldstein, G., Allen, D. N., & Deluca, J. (2019). *Handbook of Psychological Assessment, Fourth Ed*. Elsevier Science & Technology.
10. Görgens-Ekermans, G., & Roux, C. (2021). "Revisiting the emotional intelligence and transformational leadership debate: (How) does emotional intelligence matter to effective leadership?" *SA Journal of Human Resource Management*, 19(2), e1-e13. https://doi.org/10.4102/sajhrm.v19i0.1279
11. Zhu, Yang, Y., & Hsee, C. K. (2018). "The Mere Urgency Effect." *The Journal of Consumer Research*, 45(3), 673–690. https://doi.org/10.1093/jcr/ucy008
12. Drucker, P. (1967). *The Effective Executive*. Butterworth-Heinemann
13. Covey, S. (1989). *The 7 Habits of Highly Effective People: Restoring the Character Ethic*. Simon and Schuster.

14. Standaert, W., Muylle, S., & Basu, A. (2021). "Business meetings in a postpandemic world: When and how to meet virtually?" *Business Horizons*, 65(3), 267-275 https://doi.org/10.1016/j.bushor.2021.02.047
15. Yukl, G., & Fu, P. (1999). "Determinants of Delegation and Consultation by Managers." *Journal of Organizational Behavior*, Vol. 20 No. 2, pp. 219-232.
16. Joiner, T., & Leveson, L. (2015). "Effective Delegation Among Hong Kong Chinese Male Managers: The Mediating Effects of LMX." *Leadership & Organization Development Journal*, 36(6), 728-743. https://doi.org/10.1108/LODJ-11-2013-0149
17. Drescher, G. (2017). "Delegation outcomes: Perceptions of leaders and follower's satisfaction." *Journal of Managerial Psychology*, 32(1), 2-15. https://doi.org/10.1108/JMP-05-2015-0174
18. Chevrier, S., & Viegas-Pires, M. (2013). "Delegating effectively across cultures." *Journal of World Business*: JWB, 48(3), 431-439. https://doi.org/10.1016/j.jwb.2012.07.026
19. Bratton, V., Dodd, N., & Brown, F. (2011). "The Impact of Emotional Intelligence on Accuracy of Self-Awareness and Leadership Performance." *Leadership & Organization Development Journal*, 32(2), 127-149. doi:http://dx.doi.org/10.1108/01437731111112971
20. Pekaar, K., Bakker, A. B., van der Linden, D., & Born, M. (2018)." Self- and other-focused emotional intelligence: Development and validation of the Rotterdam emotional intelligence scale (REIS)." *Personality and Individual Differences*, 120, 222-233. https://doi.org/10.1016/j.paid.2017.08.045
21. Rogelberg, S., Leach, D., Warr, P., & Burnfield, J. (2006). "Not another meeting!: Are meeting time demands related to employee well-being?" *Journal of Applied Psychology*, 91, 86 –96. https://doi.org/10.1037/0021-9010.91.1.83.
22. Maxwell, J. (1995). *Developing the leaders around you: How to help others reach their full potential*. HarperCollins Leadership.
23. Pekaar, K., Bakker, A., van der Linden, D., & Born, M. (2018). "Self- and other-focused emotional intelligence: Development and validation of the Rotterdam Emotional Intelligence Scale (REIS)." *Personality and Individual Differences*, 120, 222-233. https://doi.org/10.1016/j.paid.2017.08.045
24. Rogelberg, Leach, D., Warr, P., & Burnfield, J. (2006). "Not Another Meeting! Are Meeting Time Demands Related to Employee Well-Being?" *Journal of Applied Psychology*, 91(1), 83–96. https://doi.org/10.1037/0021-9010.91.1.83

25. Baker, A., Perreault, D., Reid, A., & Blanchard, C.M. (2013). "Feedback and organizations: Feedback is good, feedback-friendly culture is better." *Canadian Psychology/Psychologie Canadienne*, 54(4), 260-268.
26. Bracken, D.W., & Rose, D.S. (2011). "When Does 360-Degree Feedback Create Behavior Change? And How Would We Know It When It Does?" *Journal of Business and Psychology,* 26(2), 183-192.
27. Lutherans, F., & Peterson, S.J. (2003). "360-degree feedback with systematic coaching: Empirical analysis suggests a winning combination." *Human Resource Management*, 42(3), 243-256.
28. Shipper, F., Hoffman, R.C., & Rotondo, D.M. (2007). "Does the 360 Feedback Process Create Actionable Knowledge Equally across Cultures?" *Academy of Management Learning & Education*, 6(1), 33-50.
29. Thach, E.C. (2002). "The impact of executive coaching and 360 feedback on leadership effectiveness." *Leadership & Organization Development Journal*, 23(4), 205-214.
30. Whitaker, B.G., & Levy, P. (2012). "Linking Feedback Quality and Goal Orientation to Feedback Seeking and Job Performance." *Human Performance*, 25(2), 159-178. 8927
31. Baumeister, R.F., Gailliot, M., DeWall, C.N., & Oaten, M. (2006). "Self-regulation and Personality: How Interventions Increase Regulatory Success, and How Depletion Moderates the Effects of Traits on Behavior." *Journal of Personality,* 74(6), 1773-1802. https://doi.org/10.1111/j.1467-6494.2006.00428.x
32. Eby, L.T., Allen, T.D., Conley, K.M., Williamson, R.L., Henderson, T., & Mancini, V.S. (2019). "Mindfulness-based training interventions for employees: A qualitative review of the literature." *Human Resource Management Review*, 29(2), 156-178. https://doi.org/10.1016/j.hrmr.2017.03.004
33. Carey, K. B., Neal, D. J., and Collins, S. E. (2004). "A psychometric analysis of the self-regulation questionnaire." *Addictive Behaviors*. 29, 253–260. doi: 10.1016/j.addbeh.2003.08.001
34. Leider, R. (2015). *The Power of Purpose,* (3rd edition). Berrett-Koehler Publishers.
35. Covey, S. (1989). *The 7 Habits of Highly Effective People: Restoring the Character Ethic.* Simon and Schuster.
36. Standaert, W., Muylle, S., & Basu, A. (2021). "Business meetings in a postpandemic world: When and how to meet virtually." *Business Horizons,* 65(3), 267-275 https://doi.org/10.1016/j.bushor.2021.02.047

Life-Changing Habit #5
Living in Balance

"To be fully engaged, we must be physically energized, emotionally connected, mentally focused and spiritually aligned with a purpose beyond our immediate self-interest."
—JIM LOEHR[1]

OVERVIEW

Business is human. No matter what business you are in, every result achieved in the workplace ultimately comes down to someone, somewhere, doing something. Human leaders are not infallible or immune to the pressures of life and leadership. The volatile, uncertain, complex, and ambiguous world creates a crisis-driven work environment contributing to increased physical, emotional, and mental exhaustion.[2]

Too often, achieving balance in life seems more like a Disney fairytale than modern reality. Some leaders see balance as an either-or choice. They either achieve success and significance in their personal lives or achieve success and significance in their professional lives. For others, the idea of balance is never considered outside of New Year resolutions or worse, when an adverse life event happens. These leaders are caught up just living their lives.

Too often, the concept of achieving balance for a leader gets overlooked. It is a real-life example of the tale of the cobbler's children, where the cobbler is so busy making shoes for customers that the cobbler's children are neglected and have no shoes. In the workplace, leaders get caught up in the busyness of the business and often neglect to achieve balance for themselves, their team, and the organization.

Additionally, when organizations and individuals act, their solutions primarily revolve around training and development for enhancing knowledge and skills, and the emotional, physical, and spiritual health of the leader is put aside. An increasing numbers of studies suggest that equal attention needs to be given to the body, mind, spirit, and emotions to achieve sustained high performance.[3] Living in balance creates the energy leaders need to achieve success and significance in their personal and professional lives.

Defining Living in Balance

Although living in balance is not a new concept for most people, few actually make necessary changes. Change is not easy. Leaders who genuinely thrive consider success and significance as a mixture of mental, physical, emotional, and spiritual health. Like a chair with four legs, the chair becomes unstable when one leg is shorter than the others. Likewise, living in balance requires leaders to work on each area of their health. Neglecting one area creates instability. Achieving balance in life lowers work distress, increases the leader's performance capacity, happiness, contentment, and compassion.

VIRTUES OF LIVING IN BALANCE

Four practical ways (virtues) to live in balance are managing job expectations, self-care, enhancing community, and work-life boundary management.

LIFE-CHANGING HABIT #5: LIVING IN BALANCE

Managing Job Expectations

In any job, it is customary to go through periods when the workload is heavier; cyclical patterns are normal. However, unrealistic workloads for sustained periods lead to exhaustion and frustration. Effectively discerning between explicit and implicit expectations is more and more essential for living in balance in an increasingly ambiguous workplace.

Managing job expectations begins with a good understanding of the current workload and admitting that it can't and shouldn't all be done by the leader. A job analysis can reveal insight into managing expectations. Start with a list of the required functions of the position, and then those tasks needed to be completed in a given day, week, or month that are beyond the essential functions. Review the list and estimate the time and frequency associated with each item to clarify the job expectations further. Writing this list helps visualize the existing reality.

Using the list of job expectations, identify the potential for delegating, deleting, reassigning, or finding additional resources. Consider your team's strengths, their development goals, your available time, and the urgency, importance, and complexity of job expectations. Effectively, managing job expectations requires an honest self-evaluation and that of the team. Additionally, leaders need to communicate constantly and openly, anticipate but not assume, and establish goals and limits for themselves and their team.

Self-Care

Self-care is fundamental to living in balance as a leader. It ultimately doesn't matter where you start, but that you do start. Working on one aspect of self-care, such as physical exercise, can improve emotional and mental health. For example, during a run in the park, you may encounter others. This provides an opportunity to build relationships.

It's not difficult to see how the spiritual, physical, emotional, and mental domains can overlap, and simple steps can lead to significant improvements.

Being a leader in today's crisis-driven workplace is exciting on the one hand and exhausting on the other. Leaders are presented with new opportunities to stretch and grow and make a real difference in areas where they find purpose. These "crucible moments" can leave them questioning their decisions and disrupt life-changing habits, creating an imbalance. At times like these, leaders may not be aware that they are sabotaging themselves.

Self-care is not selfish behavior. Like every living thing in this world, if leaders are not continually investing in restoring and strengthening physical, mental, emotional, and spiritual health, that health is deteriorating.[4] No one in the workplace escapes this reality.

Self-care involves a wide range of activities that promote well-being. Implementing and building self-care habits leads to positive emotions, improved relationships, increased physical energy, emotional inspiration, and creativity. Self-care, by definition, ends at the point of becoming dependent on someone else for achieving personal health.[5] For example, a DIY approach would be reading a book to learn more about leadership but not specific assistance from a coach or consultant.

Every leader is different in their definition of physical, spiritual, mental, and emotional health and needs. Because leaders have different definitions of success and significance in life, it is natural that health and self-care activities will vary from leader to leader. So how do leaders navigate the new normal of a high-pressure crisis-driven workplace without self-sabotaging their joy of living in the process?

Achieving balance with self-care is an individual path. Relationships, rest, and your work environment are proven to have significant influences on well-being. Going for a walk in the park with a friend and talking about life can bring a clearer perspective during challenging times. Resting away from work can provide time for leaders to process and work through a situation with clarity. Having a clean, organized workspace can provide a sense of being in control.

Enhancing Community

A community is a group defined by a shared social identification among the members and can be a vital source of support during times of crisis. Social identity theory suggests that leaders share identity with individuals with whom they associate. And as a result, leaders are more likely to trust and influence those individuals compared to individuals and groups with which they do not associate. In conversations, leaders tend to find communication more comfortable and more productive with those they consider "us" versus "them." According to social identity theory, as individuals, leaders are more motivated to be receptive and mentally able to more fully process communications with those with whom they identify.

Like a pyramid, most organizational charts narrow at the top, providing few opportunities for a role-based shared identity. As leaders move up the corporate ladder, the life-changing habit of enhancing community requires more intentional effort. Peer advisory groups, communities of practice, and affinity groups are increasingly popular forms of leadership communities.

- Peer advisory groups typically serve as an informal board of directors for the leaders. They listen, advise, and debate through shared experiences, serving as a personal advisor.
- Similar to peer advisory groups are communities of practice (CoP). A CoP is a group with common concerns, knowledge, and experiences on a given topic. As the name implies, these communities are centered around practice, where peer advisory groups are focused on the role of the leader. Communities of practice focus on creating best practices for a narrow domain, where the members possess specific expertise.

- Affinity groups include individuals from diverse backgrounds who are interested in a shared goal. Despite sharing a common goal, many may not have the subject matter expertise to achieve the goal itself or be aware of best practices.

Shared social identity increases both help-giving and social bonding and leads to increased feelings of belonging among community members. These communities produce solidarity and support for community members. Communities generate a wide range of health benefits, including a sense of belonging, reduced depression and anxiety, trust, and increased self-esteem.[6]

Work-Life Boundary Management

Advances in technology and increasing options for work from home flexibility have blurred and tested the rigidity of boundaries between work and life. Additionally, the increasing unknowns in the workplace and world have encouraged leaders to make concessions against their historical preferences of work-life boundaries. How leaders navigate their increasingly blurred work-life boundaries threatens their personal and professional goals and affects leaders' ability to achieve balance. Managing work-life boundaries effectively makes leaders better leaders.

Does work-life separation or integration lead to achieving balance? The answer varies by individual. The preference of separation or integration is best considered as a continuum with variability across individual leaders.[7] Some leaders welcome the integration of work and become stressed when they cannot respond to work at any time of the day. Other leaders feel stressed if they get a call or email during family time. A better question is, which is best for the leader? When leaders must choose between personal or professional ambitions, both the leader and the organization may lose.

Research has revealed that blurred boundaries negatively impact the well-being[8] of leaders and employees. Leaders benefit from establishing healthy work-life boundary management habits. Not making decisions between work or life leads to personal burnout and exhaustion, affecting families and communities. However, leaders who recognize the diversity of boundary styles and support followers in managing their boundaries contribute to healthy and productive teams and organizations.

PEOPLE-PLEASER DEBORAH

Deborah was a well-liked leader, hired into the role because of her technical expertise and people orientation. She connected well with her co-workers and was brief and to the point with complex problems. Deborah was committed to excellence, yet always willing to make time for those around her.

Deborah led the talent acquisition team responsible for the hard-to-fill technology positions in her company. She had a finance background and prided herself on being a non-typical talent acquisition leader. Deborah could pull off miracles by finding the ideal candidate for a specific position. As much as it was her skill to find the right person, she also managed the hiring manager's expectations.

Deborah kept a jam-packed calendar, and yet had an open door with her team and stakeholders. Everyone knew they could drop by her office and discuss what was on their mind. The growing demands of the job and that open-door approach took their toll on Deborah's physical health. Late nights and working on the weekends were having an adverse effect. Those close to her could recognize it and tried to help protect her calendar, but her approach was that it was always going to be better in a few weeks. She never took action to make things better.

However, one day she had a breakdown at work. Her co-worker saw the danger signs, and rushed her to the hospital. After tests and hours in the hospital, she was sent home with a prescription to relax and unplug from work stress. Her open-door policy had had an unfortunate impact on her health.

But the messages for help from her work kept coming. Deborah failed to recognize the warning signs and experienced a near miss as described by her doctor. Because she was so well-liked, her inattention to her calendar and slow or absent response to email were overlooked by others. She also couldn't say no to someone dropping by her office to talk. This created some inefficiencies and limited her ability to get work done during the day. She was pushing more and more work into the evenings and weekends.

Deborah made some small changes, like scheduling working times where she would not be interrupted during the day, not drinking coffee in the evening, and going for walks with a friend during breaks at work. These subtle changes led to significant physical and emotional health improvements. They made up for the shorter workdays and fewer weekends spent on work. Deborah realized an always open-door and work-harder-and-longer approach comes at a severe personal cost.

EXAMPLES OF UNBALANCED LIVING

The bad habit of unbalanced living can be recognized by leaders mismanaging job expectations, self-sabotage, isolation, and work-life boundary mismanagement habits.

Mismanaging Job Expectations

A leader's lack of attention to job expectations, either stated or implied, results in missed expectations with consequences that range from minor frustrations to catastrophic outcomes. The art of mastering expectations is increasingly essential for executive leaders in a fast-paced, crisis-driven workplace. At a personal level, the signs include personal feelings of regret about missed opportunities, and regular feelings of not doing your best work. When leaders mismanage job expectations, their teams pay the price feeling exhausted, confused, and paralyzed in decision-making from a lack of clarity. At an organizational level, mismanaging job expectations results in decreased profitability and increased avoidable business costs.

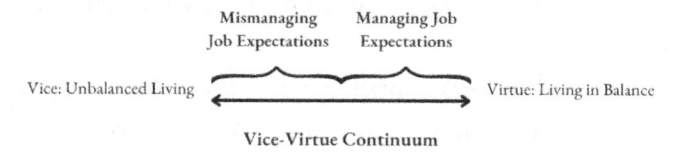

Vice: Unbalanced Living ⟵ Mismanaging Job Expectations | Managing Job Expectations ⟶ Virtue: Living in Balance

Vice-Virtue Continuum

Example Attributes and Behaviors

MISMANAGING JOB EXPECTATIONS	MANAGING JOB EXPECTATIONS
• Makes assumptions about expectations • Focuses only on explicit expectations • Saying yes to too many requests • Unrestricted accessibility	• Asks questions to clarify expectations • Uses empathic listening to reveal implicit expectations • Saying no from an informed perspective • Effective time management

Self-sabotage

Many executives experience burnout as a result of self-sabotage. These bad habits can be conscious or accidental, with consequences ranging from subtle to devastating. For example, a business owner can work tirelessly, dismissing incremental improvements and sacrificing relationships with those they love. The results of burnout range from decreased organizational performance and increased turnover of leaders to broken relationships and substance abuse.

It is easy to accidentally lose sight of physical, mental, emotional, and spiritual health in a fast-paced digital, always-on workplace. The workday is done, and you realize you rarely got up from your desk. Perhaps you worked through breaks instead of going for a walk, or you chose to eat the leftover donuts in the break room out of convenience instead of having something healthy to eat. When self-sabotage is accidental, leaders simply focus on the urgent issue of the day rather than placing achieving health on their list of priorities. Neglecting and procrastinating when it comes to taking care of yourself limits your ability to perform at your full potential.

There are many drivers contributing to the self-sabotaging actions that prevent achieving balance, including: organizational culture, past leaders' modeling, and the fear of failure.

- Unhealthy corporate cultures that emphasize working harder plus longer hours can motivate leaders to knowingly self-sabotage their health. These organizations make heroes out of leaders that sacrifice balance in their lives for the company's benefit. In these organizations, leaders purposely neglect self-care in exchange for recognition and rewards.
- Self-sabotaging habits also come from past leadership examples and mentors. The previous director, who was constantly checking and replying to emails at all hours of the day, might cause the new director to do the same. This might cause a negative impact on family relationships, when the leader thinks this is the company's expectation.
- Fear of failure emboldens the inner critic. In return, the internal critic influences executives to avoid risks instead of taking a necessary step to innovate and respond to changing environment. A failure to respond leads to potentially severe organizational consequences.

Self-sabotage leaves leaders feeling stuck and lacking self-confidence. Self-sabotage has the potential to stop momentum in a leader's life and career. Self-sabotage is like steering your boat in the wrong direction. And a lack of taking action is like letting the currents of life to push your boat to the shore.

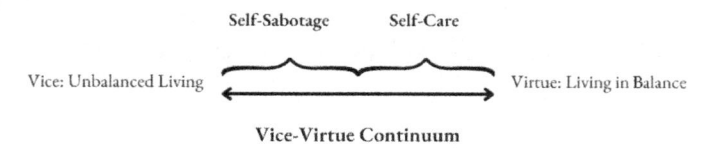

Self-Sabotage — Self-Care

Vice: Unbalanced Living ⟷ Virtue: Living in Balance

Vice-Virtue Continuum

Example Attributes and Behaviors

SELF-SABOTAGE	SELF-CARE
• Lose sight of mental, emotional, physical, and spiritual health	• Prioritize mental, emotional, physical, and spiritual health
• Expect to fail and lack confidence in achieving goals	• Expect to succeed and feel confident in your ability to achieve realistic goals
• Ignore warning signs of self-sabotage	• Take routine assessment of self-care behaviors

Isolating

Isolation is a professional hazard of being a business executive.[9] It is lonely at the top, and isolation is detrimental to achieving balance. The need to belong is human. As leaders progress up the corporate ladder, their peer community shrinks, and the potential for isolation, loneliness, and disengagement increases. The influence of power-distance amplifies the risks of isolation at the top. The impact of isolation in the workplace includes perceived reduced social support levels, lower job satisfaction, reduced effort, and increased turnover intentions. Each of these risks presents additional risks to organizational success.[10]

Research has revealed that the executive leader's isolation stems from role versus person and distance versus closeness. The role-versus-person conflict is having to hide your personality as a leader and not being true to yourself. The distance-versus-closeness conflict results from having to balance the necessary distance to perform in the executive role and, at the same time, being close enough to influence followers. Leaders are more likely to feel isolated inside and outside of work due to the demands of their position.

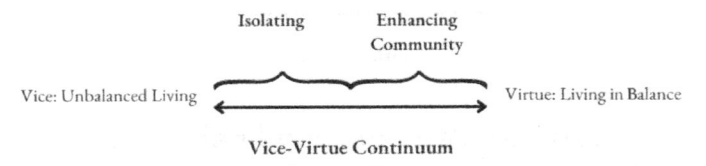

```
                        Isolating      Enhancing
                                       Community
Vice: Unbalanced Living  ⟵―――⏞―――⏞―――⟶   Virtue: Living in Balance
                         Vice-Virtue Continuum
```

Example Attributes and Behaviors

ISOLATING	ENHANCING COMMUNITY
• Avoid networking opportunities • Participate in solitary activities • Transactional relationships inside and outside of work	• Actively engage in networking inside and outside of work • Facilitate group activities • Be authentic and encourage authenticity in others

Work-Life Boundary Mismanagement

Many leaders have tossed in the towel on trying to manage work-life boundaries. This tepid response leads to increased stress, broken relationships, feelings of busyness, and disengagement. Boundary mismanagement is a failure to consider or define the cross-role needs of work and life or the inability to control work-life boundaries. When leaders fail to consider the needs of work and life, they cannot successfully schedule or manage expectations. Also, a lack of boundary control leads to feelings of regret or distress and limits the leader's success and significance.

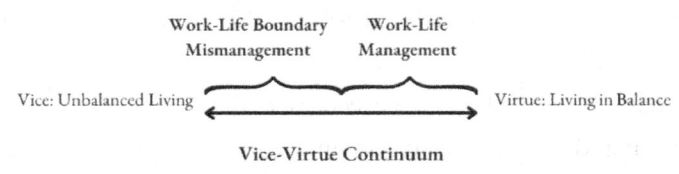

```
                 Work-Life Boundary    Work-Life
                 Mismanagement         Management
Vice: Unbalanced Living  ⟵―――⏞―――⏞―――⟶   Virtue: Living in Balance
                         Vice-Virtue Continuum
```

LIFE-CHANGING HABIT #5: LIVING IN BALANCE

Example Attributes and Behaviors

WORK-LIFE BOUNDARY MISMANAGEMENT	WORK-LIFE BOUNDARY MANAGEMENT
• Neglecting personal or professional needs	• Taking care of personal and professional needs
• Feelings of busyness	• Feelings of effectiveness
• Reacting to work-life needs and interruptions	• Managing work-life schedules and cross-role interruptions

CAUSES, CONSEQUENCES & COMPLICATIONS OF UNBALANCED LIVING

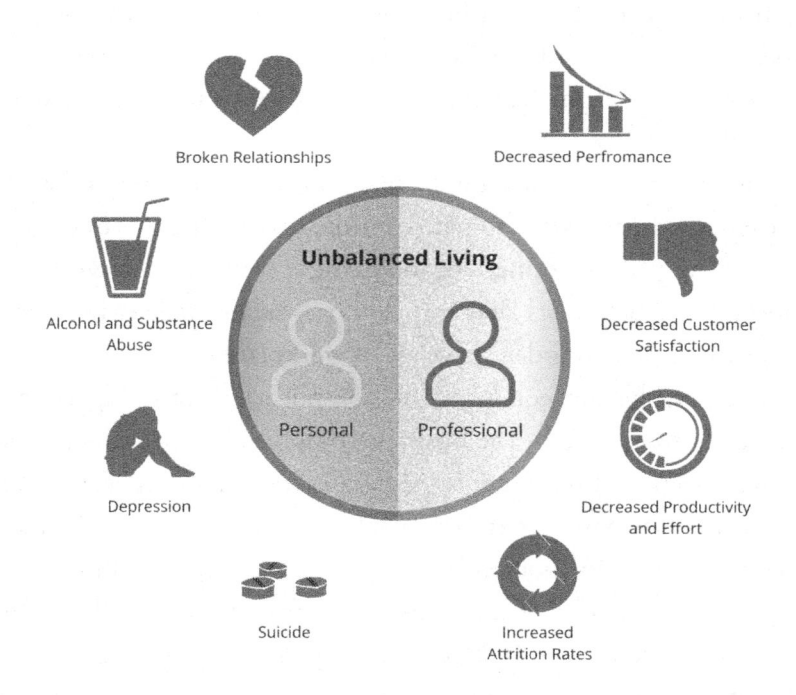

- Broken Relationships
- Decreased Perfromance
- Alcohol and Substance Abuse
- Decreased Customer Satisfaction
- Depression
- Decreased Productivity and Effort
- Suicide
- Increased Attrition Rates

Unbalanced Living — Personal | Professional

You likely have found yourself saying, "I wish I had more balance in my life," and possibly even creating New Year's resolutions each year to make a change. Many causes for unbalanced living come from inaction rather than a genuine lack of desire for balance. Making change is always difficult, but it is necessary.

Some leaders are not able to live in physical, spiritual, mental, and emotional balance in their life because they simply have never stopped to define what achieving balance means to them. There is no one-size-fits-all approach to living in balance, and leaders need to determine their own definition.

Another common cause is a lack of self-discipline or inaction. Some leaders find themselves procrastinating and not following through with prior commitments, leading to regret from failed attempts.

A lack of consistency is another factor that causes a leader to live out of balance. Often, the behaviors and actions of living healthy do not appear to be worth the effort because the benefits are not immediately visible. For instance, choosing to eat healthy is not as fun as eating that ice cream, and the benefits of eating healthy are not immediately noticeable.

Sometimes leaders lack a basic plan of action for living in balance. It is easy for the workday to get consumed with "firefighting" urgent issues and pop-up meetings. Leaders forget to plan or downplay the importance of behaviors that improve well-being. It is easy to create excuses for leaders in today's always-on workplace.

However, the consequences and complications of living a life out of balance can be severe. The business complications include increased turnover, decreased productivity, decreased customer satisfaction, and decreased performance at an organizational level. On a personal level, the complications include broken relationships, alcohol and substance abuse, depression, and even suicide at an individual leader level. Both parts impact each other. Balance can only be achieved when personal and professional are in equal portions. Living in balance includes being self-aware of strengths and weaknesses and utilizing them to the best of your ability.

LIFE-CHANGING HABIT #5: LIVING IN BALANCE

TRANSFORMATIONAL TOOLS & EXERCISES FOR LIVING IN BALANCE

How to Say No. Sometimes, you just need to say no. However, most leaders find it hard to deny legitimate requests for help. As a rule, you want to listen and make sure the requestor feels sincerely heard before responding. The following tool provides you with options and examples for how to decline effectively.

- Direct: Clearly indicate you are not able to do what has been requested. For example: "No, I won't do that." This is often the most challenging form, particularly with legitimate requests from individuals with positional power.
- Limited: Agreeing to a narrow portion of the request but declining the remainder. For example: "Absolutely, I can help with this piece of the request but will not be able to help with everything." This approach demonstrates your general willingness to help but clarifies you will only be able to help in a limited way.
- Suggested: Suggesting that the request may be incorrect but honoring their decision. This approach is helpful when you have unique insights but do not own the final decision or lack power in the relationship. The key to this approach is to provide a valuable and convincing rationale for your suggestion.
- Alternate: Offering another suggestion extends help while still declining the request. The key is to explain why this alternative is a better approach. You are still helping, just not as requested.
- Timing: Conveying your concern with timing as the rationale. This is good for legitimate requests in conflict with your work-life boundaries. For example: "I can't right now, but I could later next week."

How to Measure Burnout. ProQOL is a free, validated instrument that can be used to self-score and assess your level of burnout.[11] The tool measures your levels of compassion, satisfaction, and fatigue. Answer the following questions, considering your current situation. Using a scale of 1 = Never, 2 = Rarely, 3 = Sometimes, 4 = Often, and 5 = Very Often, select a number that honestly reflects how frequently you experienced these things over the last thirty days.

1. I am happy.
2. I feel connected to others.
3. I am not as productive at work because I am losing sleep over traumatic experiences.
4. I feel trapped by my job.
5. I have beliefs that sustain me.
6. I am the person I always wanted to be.
7. I feel worn out because of my work.
8. I feel overwhelmed because my workload seems endless.
9. I feel "bogged down" by the system.
10. I am a very caring person.

Adapted from ProQOL, The Center for Victims of Torture. www.ProQOL.org

To find your burnout level, add your scores together for the ten questions. Total scores of 22 or less indicate a low level of burnout. Scores between 23 and 41 reflect an average level of burnout for this instrument. Scores greater than 42 indicate a high level of burnout.

How to Measure and Improve Your Boundary Management. There are four main work-life boundary styles: (1) integrators, (2) cyclers, (3) separators, and (4) hybrid role firsts.

Integrators make themselves always available for work and nonwork needs. Cyclers bounce back and forth between periods of strong separation and times of full integration. Separators divide their time

LIFE-CHANGING HABIT #5: LIVING IN BALANCE

and attention between either work or non-work needs. Hybrid role first styles have a defined work first or non-work first identity and allow one identity to trump the other.

The following survey can be used to help you become more aware of your particular boundary management style. The better you understand your style, the better you can manage your work-life boundaries and achieve balance. The survey measures how you perceive boundary control, how you manage interruptions, how you balance personal and professional, technology dependence, and time for self.

Answer the following questions considering your current situation. Using a scale of 1=Strongly disagree, 2=Disagree, 3=Neither agree nor disagree, 4=Agree, and 5=Strongly agree, select a number that honestly reflects how frequently you experienced these things over the last thirty days.

1. Boundary control: I control whether I can keep my work and personal life separate.
2. Cross-role interruption: I take care of individual or family needs during work.
3. Cross-Role interruption: I work during my personal or family time.
4. Identity: I invest a large part of myself in my work.
5. Identity: I invest a large amount of myself in my family.
6. Personal time: Finding time for myself is important to my overall quality of life.
7. Technology dependence: I check my computer or hand-held device as soon as I see or hear a new message has arrived.

Adapted from Kossek (2016)[12]

Scores of one or two are considered low, scores of three suggest moderate, and scores of four to five are considered high.

- Integrators: Low personal time scores and tendencies for high technology dependence
- Separators: Moderate personal time and tendencies for low technology dependence
- Cyclers: High personal time and tendencies for high technology dependence
- Role first: High family identity scores identify as a hybrid family-first style. High work identity scores identify as a hybrid work-first style.

Generally, individuals with low scores for boundary control live out of balance. The following ideas can improve low boundary control scores:

- Using separate devices for work and non-work activities
- Using physical space to create separation between activities
- Adding time buffers to transition between your work and non-work activities
- Turning off alerts from devices during periods of time
- Blocking time in your calendar for priorities
- Partnering with an accountability partner for support
- Restricting work and non-work social media access at different times

How to Practice Self-Care. Living in balance is an individual path. Mental, physical, emotional, and spiritual domains are fundamental to achieving success and significance. The Substance Abuse and Mental Health Services Administration (SAMHSA) Creating a Healthier Life guide provides an excellent step-by-step approach with resources to help promote self-care.[13] For more information regarding the SAMHSA guide, please go to www.samhsa.gov/wellness-initiative.

How to Grow Your Network. Isolation can be a professional hazard for executives. Your professional and personal contacts become

LIFE-CHANGING HABIT #5: LIVING IN BALANCE

increasingly crucial in executive roles. Examples of potential network contacts include:

- Peers and co-workers from prior employers
- Past vendors, suppliers, and clients
- Professional connections from conferences
- Alumni from universities you attended
- Friends, neighbors, spiritual community members
- Professional organization members
- Professional service providers such as your accountant, tax preparer, or insurance provider

Adding new contacts will help you gather the information that can help you with current and future challenges. First, find contact information on those you know from your potential list of network contacts. Using LinkedIn is a great networking hack for finding connections and staying connected.

Next, you need to get organized. You will be most effective with networking when you are prepared and organized. Think through the aspects of your current position and where you could use some support. Then create three questions in advance of your meetings based on your reflection of needs.

Finally, you want to reach out and schedule a meeting. Using a short twenty-minute meeting is a great way to be respectful of your contact's time. The following agenda can help you maximize your meeting effectiveness:[14]

- Spend the first couple of minutes connecting with general conversation.
- Shift and provide a short one-minute update on what you are doing now.
- Use the next ten to twelve minutes to discuss the three questions you prepared in advance. You may want to consider asking if they

know of anyone else you should connect with to help you learn more about the topics of your questions.
- Ask if there is anything you could discuss that would help support them.
- Spend the last few minutes of the meeting saying thanks and wrapping up.
- After the meeting, it never hurts to follow up with a short thank-you note for their time and help.

KEY POINTS—LIVING IN BALANCE

- Effectively managing work-life boundaries makes leaders better leaders.
- Equal attention needs to be given to your body, mind, spirit, and emotions to achieve sustained high performance.
- Effectively managing job expectations and saying no is increasingly essential for living in balance.
- Leaders need to communicate constantly and openly, anticipate, but not make assumptions, and establish goals and limits for themselves and their team.
- Self-care is not selfish behavior.
- Every leader is different as to their needs, and therefore self-care is defined differently from leader to leader across the spiritual, physical, mental, and emotional domains.
- Communities generate a wide range of physical and mental health benefits. These include a sense of belonging, trust, increased self-esteem, and reduced depression and anxiety as well as increased well-being.
- Making choices between work or life leads to personal burnout and exhaustion, impacting families and communities.

REFLECTION QUESTIONS—LIVING IN BALANCE

- Are you truly living in balance physically, spiritually, emotionally, and mentally?

LIFE-CHANGING HABIT #5: LIVING IN BALANCE

- Are you making choices between your work-life goals? If so, where and why? Have you clearly articulated your work-life boundaries to others?
- What does self-sabotage mean to you?
- How do you feel at this moment? What makes you the happiest? What is making you feel down?
- How are your quick decisions impacting your balance? If you say yes to quick decisions, what are you saying no to?
- Do your decisions reflect your values?
- To whom in your network do you need to connect?
- Are you being authentic with others? Are you encouraging others to be authentic?

• • •

Endnotes

1. Loehr, J., & Schwartz, T. (2003). *The Power of Full Engagement: Managing Energy, Not Time, Is the Key to High Performance and Personal Renewal.* Free Press.
2. Shanafelt, T.D., & Noseworthy, J.H. (2017). "Executive Leadership and Physician Well-being: Nine Organizational Strategies to Promote Engagement and Reduce Burnout." *Mayo Clinic Proceedings*, 92(1), 129-146. https://doi.org/10.1016/j.mayocp.2016.10.004; Neal, S., Boatman, J., & Watt, B. (2021). "Global Leadership Forecast 2021." [PDF]. *Development Dimensions International, Inc.* https://media.ddiworld.com/research/GLF2021-final.pdf
3. Loehr, J., & Schwartz, T. (2003). *The Power of Full Engagement: Managing Energy, Not Time, Is the Key to High Performance and Personal Renewal.* Free Press.
4. Richards, S. (2013). "The benefits of self care." *British Journal of Healthcare Assistants,* 4(5), 246-247. https://doi.org/10.12968/bjha.2010.4.5.47976
5. Godfrey, C., Harrison, M.B., Lysaght, R., Lamb, M., Graham, I.D., & Oakley, P. (2011). "Care of self – care by other – care of other: The meaning of self-care from research, practice, policy and industry perspectives." *International Journal of Evidence-Based Healthcare,* 9(1), 3-24. https://doi.org/10.1111/j.1744-1609.2010.00196.x

6. Bowe, M., Wakefield, J.R.H., Kellezi, B., Stevenson, C., McNamara, N., Jones, B.A., Sumich, A., & Heym, N. (2021). "The mental health benefits of community helping during crisis: Coordinated helping, community identification and sense of unity during the COVID-19 pandemic." *Journal of Community & Applied Social Psychology.* https://doi.org/10.1002/casp.2520
7. Kossek, E.E., Ruderman, M.N., Braddy, P.W., & Hannum, K.M. (2012). "Work-nonwork boundary management profiles: A person-centered approach." *Journal of Vocational Behavior, 81*(1), 112-128. https://doi.org/10.1016/j.jvb.2012.04.003
8. Foucreault, A., Ollier-Malaterre, A., & Ménard, J. (2018). "Organizational culture and work-life integration: A barrier to employees' respite?" *International Journal of Human Resource Management, 29*(16), 2378-2398. https://doi.org/10.1080/09585192.2016.1262890
9. Zumaeta, J. (2019). "Lonely at the top: How do senior leaders navigate the need to belong?" *Journal of Leadership & Organizational Studies, 26*(1), 111-135. https://doi.org/10.1177/1548051818774548
10. Marshall, G., Michaels, C., & Mulki, J. (2007). "Workplace isolation: Exploring the construct and its measurement." *Psychology & Marketing, 24*(3), 195-223. https://doi.org/10.1002/mar.20158
11. Heritage, Rees, C. S., & Hegney, D. G. (2018). "The ProQOL-21: A revised version of the Professional Quality of Life (ProQOL) scale based on Rasch analysis." PLOS ONE, 13(2), e0193478–e0193478. https://doi.org/10.1371/journal.pone.0193478
12. Kossek, E.E. (2016). "Managing work-life boundaries in the digital age." *Organizational Dynamics,* 45(3), 258-270. https://doi.org/10.1016/j.orgdyn.2016.07.010
13. Department of Health and Human Services. (n.d.). "Creating a Healthier Life" [PDF]. *Substance Abuse and Mental Health Services Administration.* Retrieved January 17, 2022, from http://store.samhsa.gov/sites/default/files/d7/priv/sma16-4958.pdf
14. Ballinger, M., & Perez, N. (2012). *The 20-Minute Networking Meeting—Executive Edition: Learn to Get a Job.* Career Innovations Press.

Life-Changing Habit #6
Excelling in Management

"Your role as a leader is even more important than you might imagine. You have the power to help people become winners."
—KEN BLANCHARD[1]

OVERVIEW

Is excelling in management the same thing as excelling in leadership? These two concepts are frequently used interchangeably in business. Many people have some degree of confusion concerning the differences between leadership and management. Although similarities exist between their desired outcomes, most researchers agree they are distinctly different in achieving results.

Management involves the influence of others and the ability to align work toward shared goals. It focuses on doing things right and taking care of routine complexity in day-to-day activities. Management is concerned with strategy, structure, people, process, and reward alignment.

Adding to the confusion, some believe managers may not be good leaders, and leaders may not be good managers. There are company cultures that hold a shared belief that it is better to simply be a leader.

Managing has gotten a bad rap. In today's complex and ambiguous workplace, leaders must excel in both managing and leading to achieve success and significance. Sadly, the combination is rare.

Excelling at management is not something that happens without intentional focus and striving for something greater. A saying made popular by American football coach Vince Lombardi is that excellence is achieved in the pursuit of perfection. To excel at management requires a clear vision of the ideal and hard work toward performing at the highest level possible.

Defining Excelling in Management

Excelling in management creates a well-functioning workplace with efficient, effective, and sustainable practices ranging from administration and oversight to execution and coaching. When leaders excel in management, it results in optimal success for a company's profit, people, and community.

VIRTUES OF EXCELLING IN MANAGEMENT

Four practical ways (virtues) to excel in management include active listening, creating influence, empowering followers, and partnering.

Active Listening

Being truly heard is rare in the fast-paced digital workplace. Conversations rarely go below the surface. Additionally, the hybrid workplace has not helped. Leaders communicating with a remote workforce receive less context and visual cues due to the limitations of technology. Actively listening to employees leaves them feeling valued, affirmed, and connected emotionally. Being heard creates safety in the leader-follower relationship and is essential to establishing trust. Listening eases tensions and makes productive conflict work where resentment exists. Although being heard and understood is not commonly experienced in the workforce, listening is a leadership talent developed through practice.

Actively listening is an ability to hear and improve mutual understanding. Hearing is not a synonym for listening. When leaders actively listen, they pay attention, show interest, suspend judgment, reflect, clarify, summarize, and share to gain clarity and understanding. When leaders are practicing active listening, they are available to the other person.

Verbal, nonverbal, and empathic listening are a few of the different active listening skills:

- Active verbal listening is paraphrasing, reflecting feelings, assumption checking, and questioning skills—the words you choose to use matter. Research into the value between verbal and nonverbal active listening skills demonstrated that speaking skills are more critical for improving outcomes than nonverbal skills.
- Active empathic listening combines verbal and nonverbal active listening skills with empathy. Leaders practice this type of listening by sensing the explicit and implicit feelings being communicated. Active empathic listening is vital to innovation and maintaining close relationships.
- Active nonverbal listening refers to your body language. Eye contact, leaning forward, and an open body position all provide cues of affirmation. Avoid checking your phone, leaning back in your chair, and crossing your arms, which shows indifference and inattention. Whether intended or not, these are all cues that you are not actively listening to the employee.

The benefits of active listening are well documented for building trust and improving relationships in the work environment. When employees feel heard, they feel better about their work and their leader.

Active listening improves creativity and is a skill that cannot be outsourced. Listening for implicit and explicit needs and wants of followers and customers leads to innovations that are used and valued. Improved relationships lead to reduced stress and improved perceptions of respect that create a better environment for joint problem-solving.

The use of metaphors, slowing down, paying attention, and paraphrasing key points are helpful tips for increasing the effectiveness of active listening.

- Use metaphors. Perhaps a picture *is* worth a thousand words. Metaphors help create connections. For example, when attempting to clarify, you can ask: "Is it clear as mud?" Instead of asking: "Are you confused?"
- Slow down. Leaders are under pressure, and active listening does not typically happen in a rushed environment. The key is not to try and force a conversation into an arbitrarily scheduled time frame. Allow the option to reschedule additional time as appropriate.
- Pay attention to the speaker and your reactions. It is easy to be unaware that you are sending unintended signals. Put your technology on mute. Get curious about what they are saying, their emotions, and their reasoning. This is not the time to multi-task. Be natural and use verbal and nonverbal cues such as nodding your head or saying yes to let others know you are engaged.
- Paraphrase key points. It's like when playing catch with a ball. When the conversation is tossed to you, put what you heard into your own words to ensure you heard the key points correctly. That requires focus and attention to detail.

Creating Influence

There is broad agreement that leadership involves influencing followers toward a shared goal. Influence is the ability to change followers' thoughts, feelings, or behaviors. The notion of creating influence can be both elusive to grasp conceptually and difficult to apply in the workplace.

The lack of ability to create influence often results in leaders relying on positional power. However, frequent use of positional power comes with hidden costs to the leader and organization. In times of organizational change, leaders who rely heavily on positional power are at a loss because they no longer have their primary source of influence over others. Creating and sustaining positive influence expands possibilities for the leader, the follower, and the organization.

Leaders who create influence possess the attributes of instilling pride, going beyond themselves, building respect, projecting confidence, and having optimism about overcoming barriers to success. Logically, creating influence with others begins with living in balance. Research has demonstrated that when leaders feel exhausted or in psychological distress, they are more likely to rely on coercion.[2]

The life-changing habit of creating influence with followers involves taking the following six critical actions with followers:[3]

1. Be open about your values and beliefs. Leaders need to be clear about what is important to them and spend time sharing this with their followers. Those words, aligned with the actions of the leader, create authenticity in the leader-follower relationship.
2. Set expectations about the importance of trusting each other. Trust is fundamental to relationships. Providing help to followers before it is asked for is one way leaders can role-model the importance of trust.
3. Instill a sense of purpose in the team. Leaders that emphasize the why for the work enable teams to persist and believe—even when the work becomes difficult.
4. Promote moral decision-making. Integrity beyond reproach, striving to help others, especially when it comes at a cost, and

executing or at least striving for excellence are ways to demonstrate ethical decision-making.
5. Embrace teamwork. Adopt an approach where each team player is a needed part of the overall team and important to the success of the project.
6. Champion the best of what can be. Leadership influence is enhanced when leaders recognize and advance ideas that leverage the best of what is within the team.

There are two basic implicit or explicit questions that followers have when being asked to change. Can I do what is being asked? And, do I want to do what I am being asked? Leaders need to remove the personal, social, and structural ability and motivation barriers. The goal is to make the change(s) desired by the leader easier for followers than the undesired behaviors.[4]

Empowering Followers

Many leaders can achieve their goals and even increase company revenue. But in a world of constant change, organizations and leaders need employees who will proactively engage in problem-solving, change, innovation, and challenging the status quo. Executive leaders need followers who take charge to create a competitive advantage. However, changing and challenging the status quo is risky in most organizations. If a leader doesn't know how to empower for excellence, team morale and the business will not achieve the best of what can be.

The word empowerment has come in and out of favor when it comes to leadership. It has recently gained acceptance again within executive leadership circles, and for good reason. Leaders need committed employees. Empowerment is defined as the promotion of the skills, knowledge, and confidence necessary to take charge. Empowerment shapes feelings and actions that enhance followers' intrinsic motivation.

Understanding how to unlock intrinsic motivation is vital for leaders, followers, and organizations to achieve excellence. Leaders cannot control every situation and outcome, and followers with intrinsic motivation persist during complex and ambiguous work. They learn from failure rather than giving up.

Sadly, a common overly simplified misconception of empowerment is that leaders give away power. Empowerment without leadership is a recipe for disaster. Excelling in management requires leaders to harness empowerment by clearly articulating a compelling vision for the best of what can be at the individual, team, and organizational levels.

There is abundant research on the benefits of team effectiveness, work satisfaction, shared identity, and well-being that result from empowering followers. In addition to enhancing intrinsic motivation, empowering followers is proven to enhance autonomy, control, self-management, and confidence in team behaviors.[5] When leaders encourage followers to take the initiative with tasks such as making decisions, it increases psychological ownership, leading to a sense of responsibility and positive workplace behaviors.[6] Leaders encourage followers to take charge by applying good active listening skills, asking for input, and delegating authority.

Although there is more limited research into the most effective means for a leader to empower followers, leadership style plays a key role. Managerial practices and leadership are the primary drivers of whether followers will voluntarily take charge.

Leading from a followers-first point of view, such as servant leadership, results in a willingness to take charge, set high standards, and a devotion to each other. Trust, love, and belonging unlock the ability of the team to excel because of their differences rather than in spite of them.[7]

Partnering

Excelling in management requires careful consideration of the degree of attention and direction leaders give followers. Too much or too little attention will kill motivation and respect. Leaders are perceived as being aloof when they project a lack of emotional connection and inattention. Getting the level of attention right leads to followers who are self-reliant achievers.

Partnering with followers begins with developing high-quality relationships. These relationships unlock the potential to better understand the stated and unstated needs of followers and the given situation. Figuring out a follower's task competency level and commitment requires communication and trust found in high-quality relationships. Without a complete picture of the needs of followers, it is difficult to get the correct level of attention, leading to followers' feelings of micromanagement or absence. Also, relationships create the opportunity for feedback to understand if their understanding is accurate and, as needed, how to adjust their approach. Once leaders appropriately understand a follower's need, they must flex their approach to the proper level of support, motivation, and direction needed. Followers with less task maturity need more direction; followers with more significant experience and commitment need more supporting behaviors. When leaders appropriately match the degree of attention needed with the attention given, it leads to an improved discretionary effort, trust, and employee retention.[8] A leader's ability to engage and retain their team is essential for excelling in management.

THE ONE-MINUTE MANAGER

Jared was the president of a technology services organization that had experienced many years of success. He was known within his company for making quick decisions. Frequent changes left the organization scurrying from one new idea to the next. Employees knew if they waited long enough, Jared would move on to the next new idea. Although no one told Jared, his nickname was the "one-minute manager."

LIFE-CHANGING HABIT #6: EXCELLING IN MANAGEMENT

Jared's success was built around constantly changing his organization to meet the shifting dynamics created by advances in technology. The constant changes resulted in what he accepted as necessary complaints about change. This constant drive to take risks and find the next new idea had served Jared and the organization well in the past.

However, the industry in which his company operated was maturing, and competition was intense. Other, larger, organizations could make much more significant investments in marketing. The competition was capturing a growing percentage of the market share, and earnings were declining for Jared's company. In addition, the demand for services provided by his company was shrinking. The challenge was complex, and the company board of directors' pressure on Jared was increasingly difficult.

To meet the growing challenges, the chief strategy officer presented an idea to Jared to make a significant technology purchase and disrupt the industry with an aggressive pricing model. The new technology would introduce artificial intelligence and machine learning capability not yet widely utilized in this segment of the market. The idea was bold, and as usual, Jared quickly supported the new idea. The idea would not only be disruptive to the industry segment, but it would also be disruptive to Jared's organization.

As he and the chief strategy officer made presentations to solicit approval from the executive leadership team responsible for implementation, the idea was met with criticism rather than broad support. Feeling the pressure from his board of directors and the need for a quick response, Jared downplayed those legitimate concerns. Jared disregarded the criticism and decided to move forward, focusing on the positive aspects of the new idea. This left his direct reports feeling devalued and concerned.

Jared set an aggressive timeline for launch. The date came and was not met by the team. A second launch date was set, and again, the team missed the date. The board became increasingly concerned, as the investment for the new technology was creating additional costs. Also, the massive amount of change required amid a lean organizational structure started impacting core service levels as team members involved in the implementation felt increasingly stressed from the additional work. A few vital executive positions resigned from the company for new opportunities, and one even stepped down to try and have better work-life boundaries.

Eventually, the new idea was launched. However, the original resistance proved accurate, and the idea did not realize the anticipated benefits. The board pressed Jared over the resignations of key leaders and his judgment to move forward. Jared felt unsupported for the vision decision and left the firm.

In a crisis-driven workplace, pressure and stress had tempted Jared to take away decision authority from his team. When the risk is high, selective listening can have severe consequences for leaders, followers, and the organization.

EXAMPLES OF MICRO- AND MACROMANAGEMENT

The bad habit of micro- and macromanagement can be recognized by a leader's selective listening, use of coercion, disempowering followers, and use of a mismatched management approach.

Selective Listening

Selective listening is a costly mistake. As leaders move up the organizational chart hierarchy, they become further removed from the people who actually execute the tasks that make the organization succeed or fail. Increased organizational distance makes listening even more important and yet complex. Leaders need to know what is going on to avoid making bad decisions. Evidence is overwhelming that a lack of thorough discussion negatively impacts outcomes and organizational effectiveness. When leaders fail to listen to followers or accept what followers share, they inadvertently signal that followers are not valued. Leaders who do not listen do not inspire followers that are committed to the organization. To remain competitive and innovate, leaders need a complete picture that comes from listening to multiple points of view and acting when appropriate.

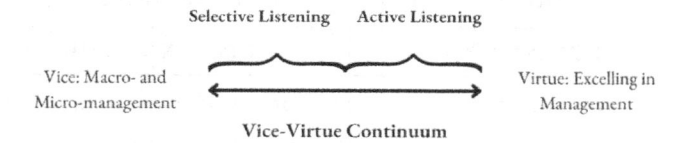

Selective Listening — Active Listening

Vice: Macro- and Micro-management ⟷ Virtue: Excelling in Management

Vice-Virtue Continuum

Example Attributes and Behaviors

SELECTIVE LISTENING	ACTIVE LISTENING
• Interested only in hearing support • Multitasking during communication, unaware of body language • Focused only on explicit verbal or written communication	• Accepting opposing views with respect and use of paraphrasing to confirm • Body language cues of affirmation • Sensing implicit or explicit feelings being communicated

Using Coercion

Coercion is an authoritarian leadership approach that relies on positional power to control employees. Coercive leaders make decisions for employees without gathering input or after disregarding the input presented. Typically, coercive leaders rely on policies and regulations to manage work. Coercive leadership eliminates innovation in a trade-off for immediate action. Coercive leadership is effective only when the leader is present and has positional authority. The lack of follower motivation created by coercive leadership diminishes organizational commitment, motivation, trust, and respect, leading to lower productivity, increased costs, and employee turnover in the long run.

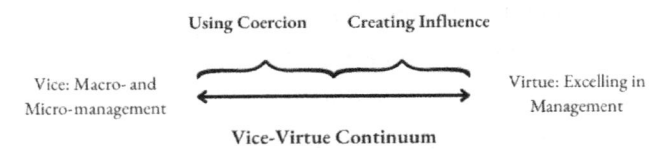

```
                    Using Coercion    Creating Influence

   Vice: Macro- and                                        Virtue: Excelling in
   Micro-management                                              Management

                         Vice-Virtue Continuum
```

Example Attributes and Behaviors

USING COERCION	CREATING INFLUENCE
• Top-down communication	• Transparent communication
• No discussion on decisions	• Encouraging trust
• Rigid structure	• Embracing teamwork
• Unchanging policies and regulations	• Championing the best of what can be

Disempowering Followers

Leaders who disempower followers stifle change and company growth, as well as create a miserable organizational culture. Typically, added pressure and stress trigger leaders to respond in ways that disempower followers. Followers who do not feel trusted do not take charge during a crisis. When leaders remove a follower's sense of self-control, responsibility, and curiosity, they disempower followers. Disempowered followers experience increased stress and lower levels of organizational commitment. Leaders that disempower followers find themselves stretched thin and usually need to be involved in every decision for their own well-being. Organizations with a disempowered workforce experience added operational costs and increased levels of employee turnover.

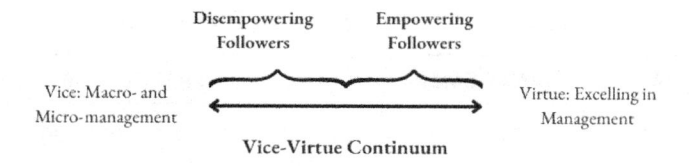

LIFE-CHANGING HABIT #6: EXCELLING IN MANAGEMENT

```
        Disempowering      Empowering
         Followers          Followers
Vice: Macro- and    ⏞      ⏞     Virtue: Excelling in
Micro-management  ←――――――――――→         Management
                Vice-Virtue Continuum
```

Example Attributes and Behaviors

DISEMPOWERING OTHERS	EMPOWERING OTHERS
• Controlling and dictating behavior	• Trusting and providing soft advice
• Criticizing and frustrating	• Encouraging autonomy
• Lack of interest and avoiding followers	• Supporting followers

Mismatched Management

Mismatched management is taking away decision-making from followers or failing to provide enough direction for their decisions. Followers experience a sense of loss of control when they are micromanaged. Conversely, when leaders abandon followers, the followers experience feelings of confusion and frustration. Mismatched management results in reduced follower morale, increased employee turnover, loss of trust, and reduced productivity and organizational commitment.

Leaders who trust their followers' competence are less likely to micromanage followers. Leaders who have high-quality relationships are more likely to match their management approach with the followers' needs. Communication is essential to avoiding misaligned management styles.

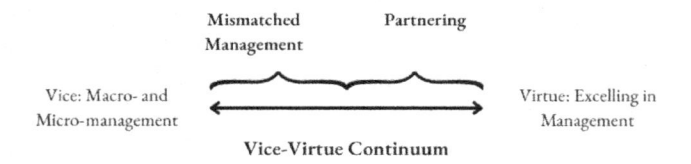

```
          Mismatched       Partnering
         Management
Vice: Macro- and    ⏞      ⏞     Virtue: Excelling in
Micro-management  ←――――――――――→         Management
                Vice-Virtue Continuum
```

Example Attributes and Behaviors

MISMATCHED MANAGEMENT	PARTNERING
• Assuming follower needs have been met • Providing a management approach based on perceived needs • The "leader knows best" approach to management	• High-quality communication and relationships • Diagnosing development and commitment needs • Directing, coaching, and supporting as needed

CAUSES, CONSEQUENCES & COMPLICATIONS OF MICRO- AND MACROMANAGEMENT

Micro- and Macromanagement

Personal | Professional

- Making Avoidable Mistakes
- Increased Employee Turnover
- Lack of Influence
- Unable to Achieve Shared Goals
- Increased Pressure
- Decreased Employee Morale
- Unable to Excel in Management
- Confusion

LIFE-CHANGING HABIT #6: EXCELLING IN MANAGEMENT

Potential causes of mismanagement are connected to both leader traits and external influences in the workplace. Detail-oriented leaders can easily fall into the trap of micromanaging employees out of a desire to better understand the details. Micromanagement does not allow for innovation. Similarly, leaders who heavily emphasize quick action can move forward without engaging followers and developing solid leader-follower relationships.

External influences that increase pressure and stress contribute to mismanagement. Perceived or real needs to make the right decision quickly can trigger leaders to take decision control away from followers. Also, within organizations with high turnover and constant change, leaders lacking high-quality leader-follower relationships find it harder to trust and give decision-making control to followers. Keeping authority but delegating responsibility never works.

Complications and consequences arising from micro- and macro-management range from minor frustrations to severe consequences. Leaders unable to excel in management struggle to influence followers and achieve shared goals. Not focusing on doing things right and taking care of routine complexity results in avoidable mistakes and added costs to the business. Confusion, frustration, lower morale, lower organizational commitment, increased employee turnover, and decreased discretionary effort are some of the organizational complications that arise from micromanagement and macromanagement. In addition to the pressure to increase efficiency and reduce costs, leaders unable to excel in management find themselves pulled in many different directions. They are either not close enough or too close to the business' operations. Both scenarios threaten the ability of a leader to achieve success and significance.

TRANSFORMATIONAL TOOLS & EXERCISES FOR EXCELLING IN MANAGEMENT

How to Encourage Others to Use Active Listening: Everyone has been in a situation where they don't feel heard. The following are some strategies you can try to help bring about the change you want to see:

- **Find common ground.** Whether you are getting to know a person or engaging a leader you report to on a complicated topic, starting with something you share in common can help create interest.
- **Be a role model.** Being the change you want to see in the world is a powerful tool for influencing change in the workplace. Don't be the one wanting to be listened to but unwilling to listen. Look in the mirror and assess how you are doing before trying to fix someone else.
- **Let them know.** Often it is not a lack of desire as to why someone is not using active listening skills. If you decide to provide this feedback, you want to use an "I" statement, such as "I don't feel like you are hearing me."

How to Develop Your Active Listening Skill. If you are ready to invest some energy into developing your active listening skills, the following list of ideas is compiled from various research studies on active listening.

- **Daily reflection.** Honestly reflect and assess daily how you are doing. Reflect on specific conversations to identify what went well and what still needs improvement. Specifically, focus on how well you paid attention, showed an interest, suspended judgment, reflected on what you heard, clarified understanding, summarized, and shared with others to gain clarity and better understanding.

LIFE-CHANGING HABIT #6: EXCELLING IN MANAGEMENT

- **Find a mentor.** A mentor should be someone who is a skilled active listener. This will be someone who can role-model and help ask good, reflective questions to help you learn.
- **Find an accountability partner.** An accountability partner can be someone who is also working on building their active listening skills—or they could already be skilled. The key is that they can observe you and catch you either using or not applying active listening skills.
- **Focus.** Consciously choose to focus on building your active listening skills. Don't expect to grow these skills while your focus is elsewhere.
- **Experiential practice.** Like building physical endurance and strength, you can build active listening skills with training. Use blended experiential methods that require learning by doing. Active listening is influenced by the context of the conversation and cues that are best learned by doing. Don't just rely on reading about active listening.

How to Measure Your Preferred Leadership Approach. The Leader Behavior Analysis II 360 can be used to understand your preferred leadership approach and improve your adaptability with input from followers, peers, and your leader. The instrument is based on questions about how you act in various situations. The questions align with the four Hersey Blanchard Situational Leadership styles of directing, coaching, facilitating, and observing. The Situational Leadership model shows that, depending on the follower's situation or task, one of the four styles is a better match to the follower's needs than another.

For more information regarding this assessment, contact The Ken Blanchard Companies at www.kenblanchard.com.

KEY POINTS—EXCELLING IN MANAGEMENT

- Leadership and management are similar but distinctly different in how outcomes are achieved.
- Management is focusing on doing things right and is concerned with taking care of routine complexity in day-to-day activities.
- Excelling in management creates a well-functioning workplace with efficient, effective, and sustainable practices ranging from administration and oversight to execution.
- Being truly heard is rare in the fast-paced digital workplace.
- Actively listening is your ability to hear and improve mutual understanding.
- The use of metaphors, slowing down, paying attention, and paraphrasing key points are helpful tips for overcoming your barriers to active listening.
- Leaders who create influence can go beyond themselves, build respect, instill pride, and project confidence and optimism about overcoming barriers to success.
- Leaders encourage followers to take charge by applying active listening skills, asking for input, and delegating authority.
- Excelling in management requires careful consideration of the degree of attention and direction leaders give followers.

REFLECTION QUESTIONS—EXCELLING IN MANAGEMENT

- Thinking back to your last conversation, what were the explicit and implicit feelings communicated to you?
- Are you listening to the nonverbal cues others are sending or avoiding them?
- How do you view your followers' level of commitment and development on their assigned tasks? Would they agree with your assessment?

LIFE-CHANGING HABIT #6: EXCELLING IN MANAGEMENT

- Are you treating followers unequally—by treating them all the same—concerning how you direct, coach, or provide support?
- How often do you use metaphors when communicating with others?
- What are your values and beliefs? Have you shared them with your followers?
- Do you engage in conversations with followers to discover what they believe is the best of what can be for themselves, the team, and the organization?
- Rank your follower relationships from the most trusting to the least trustful.
- What is the difference between the top-rated relationship and bottom-rated relationship? How can you improve trust in each relationship?
- Are you creating an environment where followers are willing to take risks?

• • •

Endnotes

1. Blanchard, K. (2007). *Heart of a Leader: Insights on the Art of Influence.* David C. Cook Publishing Company. p.13
2. Byrne, A., Dionisi, A.M., Barling, J., Akers, A., Robertson, J., Lys, R., Wylie, J., & Dupré, K. (2014). "The depleted leader: The influence of leaders' diminished psychological resources on leadership behaviors." *The Leadership Quarterly, 25*(2), 344-357. https://doi.org/10.1016/j.leaqua.2013.09.003
3. Sosik, J.J., & Jung, D. (2018). *Full Range Leadership Development: Pathways for People, Profit, and Planet* (2nd ed.). Routledge. https://doi.org/10.4324/9781315167206
4. Patterson, K., Grenny, J., Maxfield, D., McMillan, R., & Switzler, A. (2013). *Influencer* (Second ed). McGraw-Hill Professional Publishing.
5. Li, S.L., He, W., Yam, K.C., & Long, L.R. (2015). "When and why empowering leadership increases followers taking charge: A multilevel examination in China." *Asia Pacific Journal of Management, 32*(3), 645-670. https://doi.org/10.1007/s10490-015-9424-1

6. Edelmann, C.M., Boen, F., & Fransen, K. (2020). "The Power of Empowerment: Predictors and Benefits of Shared Leadership in Organizations." *Frontiers in Psychology*, 11, 582894-582894. https://doi.org/10.3389/fpsyg.2020.582894
7. Leavy, B. (2020). "Frances Frei and Anne Morriss: The dynamics of empowering leader/follower relationships." *Strategy & Leadership*, 48(6), 27-33. doi:http://dx.doi.org/10.1108/SL-09-2020-0125
8. Zigarmi, D., & Roberts, T.P. (2017). "A test of three basic assumptions of Situational Leadership® II Model and their implications for HRD practitioners." *European Journal of Training and Development*, 41(3), 241-260. https://doi.org/10.1108/EJTD-05-2016-0035

Life-Changing Habit #7
Mastering Difficult Conversations

> "Daring greatly means the courage to be vulnerable. It means to show up and be seen. To ask for what you need. To talk about how you're feeling. To have the hard conversations."
> —BRENÉ BROWN[1]

OVERVIEW

Leadership is a relationship, and communication is fundamental in every relationship. However, there are some conversations that all leaders approach with great apprehension. Just the thought of the conversation leads to feelings of anxiety and stress that can ruin an evening, day, or even an entire weekend. Leaders are tempted to avoid these difficult conversations but know they won't go away. Difficult conversations are vital to successful relationships and the results by which leaders are judged.

Difficult conversations come in all shapes and sizes. Stress and pressure associated with these conversations make leaders vulnerable to mistakes and further increase the conversations' difficulty. Sometimes the topic is awkward, and that is why it is difficult. Other times the dialogue is related to a tense situation, with severe consequences for both leader and follower. Some topics are simply complex and ambiguous, making the ability to have the conversation challenging for both parties. Ultimately, whether the conversation is perceived as difficult is dependent on the viewpoint of both parties engaged in the conversation.

No leader-follower relationship stays constant. Like all natural systems, they evolve, either on purpose or by accident. When leaders avoid difficult conversations or do not handle them well, it can lead to relationship strife, failure, and missed growth opportunities. Mastering difficult conversations create the best possible outcomes for the leader, the leader-follower relationship, the team, and the company.

Defining Mastering Difficult Conversations

Leaders who master difficult conversations embrace getting comfortable with the uncomfortable. Mastering those conversations involves leaning into the conversation's anxiety and complexity with a heightened sense of urgency and awareness of verbal, nonverbal, and empathic cues being sent and received. Leaders who master difficult conversations can identify the explicitly stated and implied needs to benefit both leaders and followers. Successful conversations reduce strife in the workplace and lead to enhanced morale, employee engagement, organizational commitment, and desired behaviors.

VIRTUES OF MASTERING DIFFICULT CONVERSATIONS

Three practical ways (virtues) to master difficult conversations are being vulnerable, creating productive conflict, and focusing on what matters most.

Being Vulnerable

Regardless of leadership level or amount of experience, all leaders struggle with the tension of being vulnerable. In difficult conversations, followers

LIFE-CHANGING HABIT #7: MASTERING DIFFICULT CONVERSATIONS

want to know their leader cares about them. But concerns about managing personal perceptions often keep leaders from showing vulnerability in the workplace. And when leaders are guarded in difficult conversations, it promotes distrust.

Although leaders are expected to convey competence, confidence, and power, followers already know leaders are not perfect. Being vulnerable as a leader in difficult conversations requires courage. Leaders must learn to be comfortable without having all the information wanted or needed. Leadership vulnerability involves the willingness to take risks that might end in failure—or create the best of what might be in the organization.

Practicing vulnerability as a leader involves checking personal motivation, vision, and paradigm (MVP) before having a difficult conversation.[2]

- **Motivation.** Is your motivation about caring for others first? Or is your motivation being right? Reasons for a conversation matter. Without a positive reason, it is unlikely the conversation will lead to positive changes.
- **Vision.** How do you see the result of the conversation going? Is it the best of what might be? Or is what you see a list of all the things that could go wrong? Anticipating a positive step in the journey provides a sense of purpose and direction to inspire you to do your best and achieve success.
- **Paradigm.** When the lens through which you perceive the difficult conversation is off, your results will turn out poorly. Is your paradigm for the difficult conversation that real transparent conversation will provide the best foundation for a healthy culture and your relationship? Or is your paradigm that it is best to avoid difficult conversations because you need to manage your image?

Often, the word "weakness" is considered a synonym for vulnerability. However, being vulnerable takes strong leadership and creates a significant amount of influence in the leader-follower relationship. Vulnerability is a courageous choice.

Vulnerability in a difficult conversation is best modeled by the leader first. When leaders display vulnerability in a conversation, it establishes trust and safety for followers. It opens the door to productive interaction and the potential for positive change. A display of openness by the leader encourages followers, in turn, to take risks and leads to improved communication, productivity, collaboration, innovation, relationships, and employee retention. Followers want to see that their leader cares for them and is open to learning new ideas without judgment.

There is no one complete checklist of actions that leaders can use to show vulnerability in every difficult conversation. However, the following list of leadership habits is compiled from proven research on mastering difficult conversations:

- **Being transparent.** Keep the conversation genuine, especially if it involves your mistakes. This does not mean sharing personal secrets. It means metaphorically inviting those you are speaking with into the front door of your house rather than making them stand on the doorstep and talk with you from behind your "screen door" of image management. Being transparent pertains to both the logical rationale aspects of the conversation as well as your feelings about the other person and the conversation.
- **Putting followers first.** It is when you care so much about your followers and the desired outcome of the conversation that you are willing to risk failing. It is not about winning or having the best answer. Putting others first doesn't mean thinking less of yourself; it is admitting a challenge exists and thinking of yourself less.
- **Asking for feedback and being willing to learn.** Vulnerability is about being open to other points of view and desiring to listen and learn. When asking for feedback, it is essential to remember that it is a gift given. When delivering a tough message that has

not been shared before, it can be best to be direct and to the point and then offer to discuss later. This allows time for the message to be processed analytically and emotionally at the follower's pace before you ask for feedback.
- **Demonstrating selfless love.** Selfless love is to will the good of another. As a leader, being vulnerable always requires showing self-awareness, empathy, and compassion—not speaking from positional power. Self-awareness improves your communication clarity and ability to understand multiple perspectives. Empathy helps you listen and understand how others are feeling, and compassion inspires actions that are helpful.
- **Taking action.** Balancing the need to prepare with the need to take action is important. Difficult conversations are costly when neglected. It is easy to get caught in a trap of waiting for more information, which leads to procrastination. In the most difficult conversations, you may never have all the information you would like.

Productive Conflict

Conflict is common in life and work. According to a survey of five thousand full-time employees in nine countries, 85 percent of employees deal with conflict at work. This same study found that U.S. workers spend more than 2.5 hours per week in a conflict.[3] But productive conflict is rare. Most people tend to have negative feelings associated with the word "conflict." However, conflict is not always referring to aggressive confrontations or arguments. Conflict could mean a heated argument or a minor difference of opinion. The distinction often lies in the issue's importance and the amount of energy put into a conversation.

Conflict is not a sign of failure, but it becomes something worse when it is avoided or ignored. Effectively managing conflict affects relationships, well-being, job satisfaction, and productivity. Of course, it is natural to want to minimize workplace conflict. Still, it is necessary to manage conflict and realize that it can have many positive outcomes. Leaders who understand the difference between creating conflict that works and causing strife that damages team results and relationships can master difficult conversations.

Productive conflict is an open exchange of differing goals or interests. Parties feel equally heard, respected, and unafraid to voice dissenting opinions to reach a mutually agreeable resolution. Even though conflict may be uncomfortable, it is productive to have ideas challenged to learn and grow.

Productive conflict requires a healthy workplace culture and a strong commitment and dedication from leaders and everyone within the workplace. Conflict impacts more than those who recognize the conflict. Also, it is essential to realize that our reactions to conflict can result in either positive or negative consequences.

When it comes to productive conflict, understanding what not to do in a difficult conversation is just as important as understanding what to do. The following are some tips to keep from mismanaging conflict:

- Don't wait around and do nothing. If a conflict is left unresolved, it will escalate over time, with win-lose outcomes.
- Don't let your bias and stories drive your solution to the issue. We all have biases, and when conversations turn difficult, it is more difficult to pause and reflect on the situation and people involved before moving to solutions. Don't try to be correct and impose your perfect solution. A key to avoiding mistakes is less about thinking about what is said and more about hearing the follower. Listen for verbal, nonverbal, and empathic cues in the conversation.
- Model taking responsibility and offering a sincere apology and forgiveness. Even productive conflict has the potential to produce feelings of anxiety.[4] When leaders exert an effort to

LIFE-CHANGING HABIT #7: MASTERING DIFFICULT CONVERSATIONS

restore damaged relationships, they increase the willingness and likeliness of followers to cooperate and engage in future productive conflict.
- Don't approach workplace conflict without a plan. As the saying goes, if you fail to plan, you plan to fail. Take time to prepare a productive conflict approach, so you are not reacting without thinking.

Disagreements do not have to be divisive. What you choose to do or not do will largely determine if you achieve productive conflict. Avoiding conflict takes time and energy. A conflict avoided will only make a difficult conversation more costly for those involved and impact the company. Commit and act. Like rapids in a river, there will be times of conflict in the workplace. Also, there will be times like an eddy in a stream that is calm. Both are natural and healthy parts of a river and every workplace. The following are a few tips for what leaders should do for managing productive conflict in the workplace:

- Develop a generic plan for how to approach conflict in your workplace. It's best to consider this conflict plan ahead of the time needed. A good method of approach should include answers for how to handle the *what*, *when*, *where*, *how*, and *why* specific to conflict situations and those involved.
- Provide training for leaders and employees on effectively managing productive conflict in the workplace. Training and development efforts should go beyond a one-time training event.
- Encourage healthy relationships and all employees taking ownership in resolving non-productive workplace conflict. Foster a sense of shared social identity with followers. Leaders and followers are more comfortable and feel safer communicating with those considered "us" versus "them." Create a culture of accountability for productive conflict that starts with leaders.

Focusing on What Matters Most

Many leaders struggle with getting clarity on what matters most in a difficult conversation. With the complexity and fast-paced nature of the workplace, leaders often stop at having just a simple conversation. Pausing to identify the right conversation may seem like a luxury. But in difficult conversations, overlooking this step comes at a cost. When a leader fails to focus on what matters most, it increases the likelihood of pitfalls. The benefits of this step far outweigh the costs. Focusing on what matters most defuses the emotional intensity of the conversation, improves solution effectiveness, reduces the need to repeat the discussion in the future, and improves the leader-follower relationship.

Leaders who master difficult conversations create a gap between action and response to choose what conversation matters most. It is easy to become triggered by emotions into immediately having a difficult conversation. Like a ship approaching an iceberg, what alerts a leader of a potential problem is what is seen, but what lies below the surface presents the greatest cause for concern. A specific behavior may be the visible cause for concern in the workplace, but a follower's virtues and character below the surface matter most. Of course, not every difficult conversation needs to include a discussion on virtues. But words inspire actions and reminders of who we are and how we want to be impacts the right conversation.

In addition to choosing the right issue for difficult conversations, it is essential to select the right level. There are three basic levels of conversations that leaders have:[5]

- **Level 1:** The first level is a conversation about a specific issue, such as showing up late for a meeting and exploring the cause. A simple conversation in passing may be appropriate.
- **Level 2:** The second level is a conversation about a pattern of topics, such as showing up late for several meetings. Meeting in private is best to discuss the reasons for having this conversation.

LIFE-CHANGING HABIT #7: MASTERING DIFFICULT CONVERSATIONS

- **Level 3:** The third, and most serious level, is the health of the leader-follower relationship. These difficult conversations are typically the result of a lack of trust, concerns about competence, or loss of respect in the follower.

When a conversation begins to feel frustrating or progress on the issue is not being made, it is an excellent time to reconsider the conversation's level. Leading with the life-changing habit of focusing on what matters most makes a profound difference in mastering difficult conversations.

FINDING COURAGE

Sophia was a high-performing director in an organization she loved. She was a wonderful person, liked by everyone, and had been with the company for several years. Sophia appreciated her leader, Will, the vice president of sales. He took a chance on Sophia several years earlier by promoting her into the director position she now held. Sophia appreciated him giving her a chance and how he encouraged her work. There were strong feelings of mutual respect.

Due to a recent crisis in the marketplace, the organization had to make some difficult decisions to downsize. Those decisions impacted Will's department significantly, and he was not happy about the reductions. Furthermore, because of the downturn in profits, the director of marketing left and went to work for a competitor. These actions weighed heavily on Will and Sophia, who were both feeling the stress.

Out of her desire to see her company and leader succeed, Sophia volunteered to fill the director of marketing role for one year, in addition to her current responsibilities. They were both aware of the increased work, but in desperation and a desire to see Sophia continue to develop, Will agreed. Also, he was able to redirect some of the funding saved from the reduced salary costs to Sophia's base salary.

Immediately, Sophia's teams were feeling the effects of her decision. Her old unit had to take on more responsibilities due to her limited capacity. Her new marketing team had to pick up more due to her lack of technical capability. Sophia's performance was slipping, and both teams were beginning to feel burned out as a result of Sophia and Will's decision.

After a few short weeks, it became apparent to Sophia that this new one-year stretch assignment had overextended her capacity and technical capabilities. She knew Will was already feeling stressed, and she believed her news would make him feel even worse.

The seriousness of Sophia's performance and her team members' burnout required action. After a few days, she worked up the courage to decide to go back on her written commitment to Will. All that remained was having the difficult conversation at her next one-to-one meeting with Will.

The day of the meeting came, but Sophia couldn't find the courage to break the news to Will. Rather than face the music, she procrastinated, but the stress only intensified. Sophia finally scheduled an appointment with Will to discuss the stretch assignment.

The time came for the meeting, and Sophia had rehearsed how she would break the news to Will. Before she could say anything, Will said to her, "I know." They had both recognized the assignment was not a good fit, and both avoided the difficult conversation. Will had not wanted to take away the opportunity from Sophia, and Sophia had not wanted to have the conversation because of the impact on Will.

Thankfully, Sophia and Will learned a valuable lesson about the importance of having a difficult conversation before the teams and organization experienced severe consequences. They reassigned and regrouped, strengthening their team's commitment by allowing the work to be better distributed. The outcome allowed both Will and Sophia to act on the situation honestly and succinctly—with a positive result.

EXAMPLES OF MISMANAGING DIFFICULT CONVERSATIONS

The bad habit of mismanaging difficult conversations can be recognized by leaders being guarded, mismanaging conflict, and avoiding what matters most in difficult conversations.

Being Guarded

Often, leaders fear being vulnerable in front of their followers and work tirelessly always to have an answer, even an incorrect one. However, a guarded approach rarely builds a leader's influence. At the heart of social connection are vulnerability and authenticity.[6] Leaders without the courage to be themselves in front of their team miss an opportunity to establish a human connection. When leaders are guarded in front of followers, it promotes distrust and disconnection. A lack of trust creates an unhealthy workplace culture that negatively affects the leader-follower relationship, engagement, productivity, and organizational commitment.

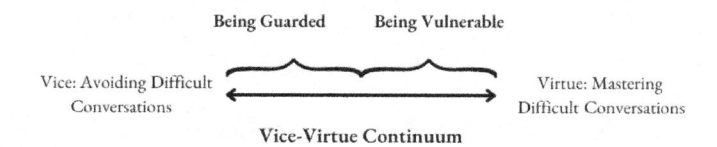

Being Guarded — Being Vulnerable

Vice: Avoiding Difficult Conversations ←——————→ Virtue: Mastering Difficult Conversations

Vice-Virtue Continuum

Example Attributes and Behaviors

BEING GUARDED	BEING VULNERABLE
• Being inauthentic	• Courage to be yourself
• Professional distance	• Emotional exposure
• Managing perceptions and image	• Risk-taking and accepting uncertainty in relationships

Mismanaging Conflict

Despite best intentions, sometimes personalities, heavy workloads, lack of respect, or cultural differences can lead to conflict and difficult conversations. Mismanaging conflict produces too much, not enough, or non-productive conflict. Mismanaging conflict impacts well-being, decreases productivity, and increases turnover. Non-productive conflict is an exchange of conflicting or differing ideas. This conflict arises when the real issues are not discussed, and attention is placed on trivial matters. This leads to parties not feeling equally heard, respected, and afraid to voice dissenting opinions.

Avoiding conflict and tolerating drama creates a toxic and untrustworthy work environment. Avoiding conflict escalates tensions, which leads to strife. While productive conflict is healthy, too much is disruptive and creates unnecessary friction among followers. A high-conflict workplace leaves the organization worse off. Followers respect leaders who act responsibly with regard to conflict.

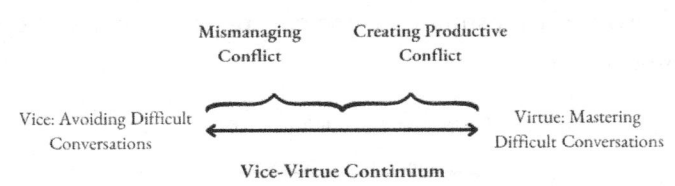

	Mismanaging Conflict	Creating Productive Conflict	
Vice: Avoiding Difficult Conversations	←	→	Virtue: Mastering Difficult Conversations

Vice-Virtue Continuum

Example Attributes and Behaviors

MISMANAGING CONFLICT	CREATING PRODUCTIVE CONFLICT
• Being guarded	• Being transparent
• Unwilling to learn from others	• Accepting feedback
• Lack of empathy or compassion	• Demonstrating selfless love
• Creating unnecessary conflict or avoiding necessary conflict	• Acting responsibly

LIFE-CHANGING HABIT #7: MASTERING DIFFICULT CONVERSATIONS

Avoiding What Matters Most

It is easier for most leaders to talk about surface issues than what matters most in a relationship. However, difficult conversations can be accidentally created by having the wrong discussion. When what matters most is the leader-follower relationship or a pattern of problems, but the conversation is about showing up late for a recent meeting, it can lead to increased frustration and failure to resolve concerns. Avoiding what matters most in a difficult conversation increases emotional intensity, creates frustrations for both parties, and results in repeated ineffective discussions.

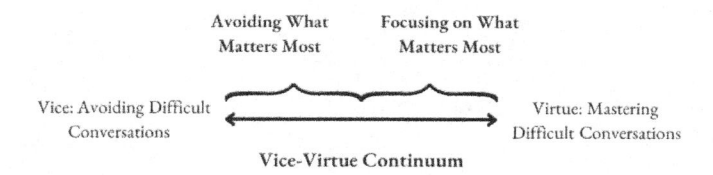

Avoiding What Matters Most — Focusing on What Matters Most

Vice: Avoiding Difficult Conversations ⟷ Virtue: Mastering Difficult Conversations

Vice-Virtue Continuum

Example Attributes and Behaviors

AVOIDING WHAT MATTERS MOST	FOCUSING ON WHAT MATTERS MOST
• Respond hastily to conflict • Focus on behaviors • Chooses content over relationship conversations	• Create a gap between action and response • Considers the role of virtues and character • Chooses relationships and patterns over content conversations

CAUSES, CONSEQUENCES & COMPLICATIONS OF MISMANAGING DIFFICULT CONVERSATIONS

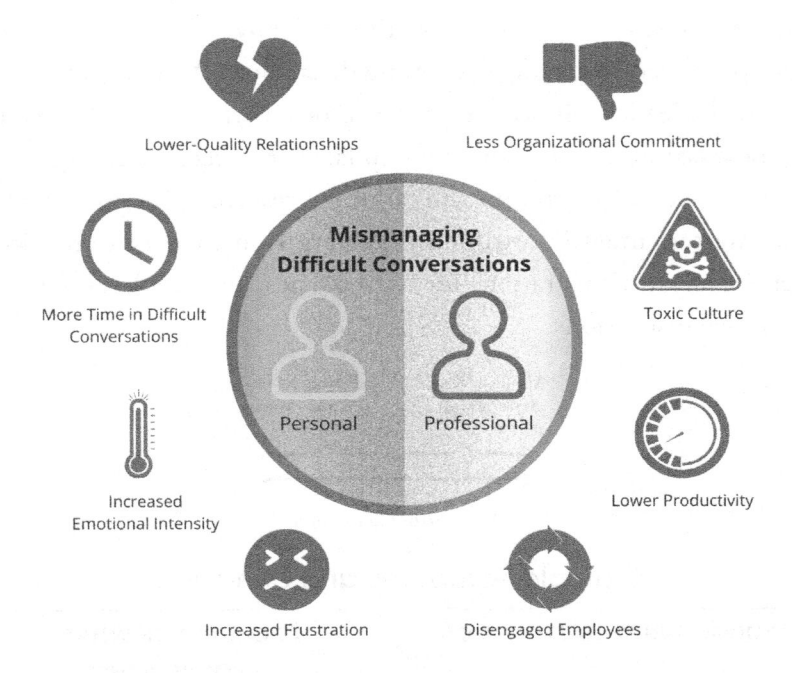

Lower-Quality Relationships
Less Organizational Commitment
More Time in Difficult Conversations
Mismanaging Difficult Conversations — Personal | Professional
Toxic Culture
Increased Emotional Intensity
Lower Productivity
Increased Frustration
Disengaged Employees

Leaders do not set out to mismanage difficult conversations. Often, difficult conversations are mismanaged due to apathy toward a given situation or the influence of intense emotions surrounding an issue like fear, anger, or frustration in the workplace. When leaders fear transparency, they become guarded, leading to mismanaged conversations. Also, when leaders ignore conflict, relationships become strained, increasing the complexity and severity of an issue and making an already tricky conversation more challenging.

Occasionally, mismanaged difficult conversations are caused by a leader's traits and the company culture. Mastering those conversations requires leaders to be vulnerable, to listen, and to have empathy and a willingness to be direct with followers. When leaders have personality traits characterized as manipulative or antisocial or have a heightened

LIFE-CHANGING HABIT #7: MASTERING DIFFICULT CONVERSATIONS

desire to be liked or are self-involved, they are less likely to master difficult conversations.

Additionally, an unhealthy workplace culture can make difficult conversations even more difficult. In workplaces where employees are required to always be correct or never fail, they are less likely to demonstrate the vulnerability needed to master difficult conversations. Toxic cultures strain relationships, limit trust, and complicate communication.

Complications and consequences arising from mismanaging difficult conversations range from minor frustrations to severe consequences for the leader, team, and organization. Leaders unable to master difficult conversations experience greater frustration, spend more time in difficult conversations, and are not trusted. Organizations and teams experience increased emotional intensity, lower-quality relationships, toxic company culture, disengaged employees, lower productivity and efficiency, and less organizational commitment.

TRANSFORMATIONAL TOOLS & EXERCISES FOR MASTERING DIFFICULT CONVERSATIONS

How to Develop Your Productive Conflict Skills. One of my favorite tools for assessing a leader's expectations and desires in conflict situations is the Thomas-Kilmann Conflict Mode Instrument (TKI). It is quick to complete and easy to understand for teams and individuals at any organizational level. The instrument describes behavior along the axes of assertiveness to satisfy personal concerns and cooperativeness to meet the other person's concerns. Using the TKI helps team members get to know each other and identify potential challenges and strategies to manage issues constructively before a conflict arises.

The TKI model describes five types of conflict and the methods for successfully managing conflict: (1) competing, (2) collaborating, (3) compromising, (4) avoiding, and (5) accommodating.

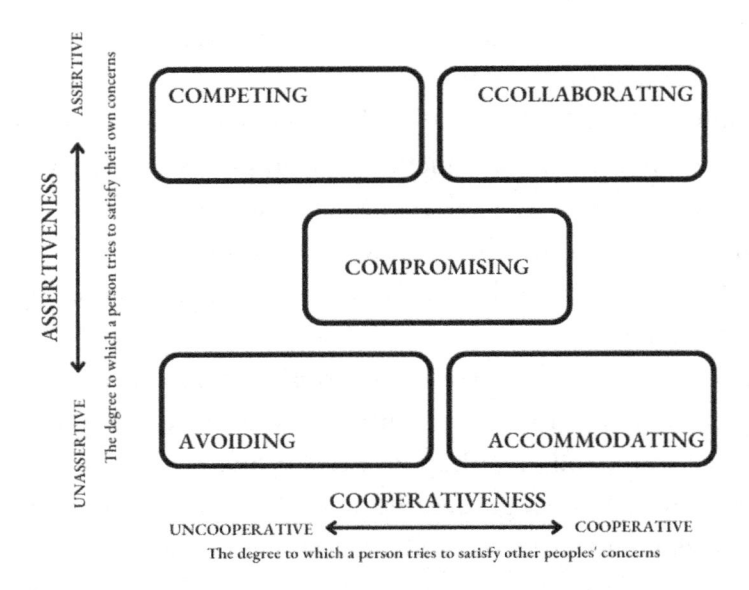

```
                              ASSERTIVE
                    ┌─────────────┐         ┌─────────────┐
                    │  COMPETING  │         │ CCOLLABORATING │
                    └─────────────┘         └─────────────┘
    ASSERTIVENESS
                           ┌─────────────────┐
                           │  COMPROMISING   │
                           └─────────────────┘

                    ┌─────────────┐         ┌─────────────┐
                    │  AVOIDING   │         │ ACCOMMODATING │
    UNASSERTIVE     └─────────────┘         └─────────────┘
                              COOPERATIVENESS
                    UNCOOPERATIVE  ←——→  COOPERATIVE
```

Note: Conflict model adapted from Schaubhut (2007).[7]

For more information regarding this assessment, contact The Myers-Briggs Company at www.cpp.com/TKI.

How to Avoid Difficult Conversation Control Traps. Sometimes the volatility, complexity, or legality of an issue can cause leaders to micromanage the conversation and not be as authentic or transparent as needed to master a difficult conversation. The following are two common traps to avoid:

- **Micromanaging the flow of communication.** In response to the intensity of emotion or legality surrounding a conversation, leaders can micromanage communication and limit their effectiveness. Followers want to see and hear directly from their leaders. Followers want to know leaders are human and share in the difficulty of the conversation issue. It takes courage to press into these issues.

LIFE-CHANGING HABIT #7: MASTERING DIFFICULT CONVERSATIONS

- **Micromanaging Emotions.** It is often easier to focus on the facts of the conversation, especially at the executive level. However, people process communication from an intrapersonal to interpersonal perspective, and it is important to listen and communicate verbal, nonverbal, and empathic cues. Sharing emotions is fundamental to being vulnerable, building trust, and establishing social connections needed to master difficult conversations.

It can be lonely at the top. Engaging an executive coach to have someone to listen, be a thought partner, and turn ideas into action during difficult conversations can be a powerful tool to break the difficult conversation control traps.

How to Gauge and Develop Your Difficult Conversation Competence. To master difficult conversations you first must be willing to have the difficult conversation. If everyone agrees with your ideas, you are not able to reach new and better ideas. The following short self-assessment can be used to quickly gauge how likely you are to engage in an argument. It is important to note that an argument as referenced in this instrument is different from verbal aggression that is destructive to relationships.

Instructions: Using the following argumentativeness scale, indicate how often the statement is true for you. 1 = almost never true, 2 = rarely true, 3 = occasionally true, 4 = often true, 5 = almost always true.

1. While in an argument, I worry that the person with whom I am arguing will form a negative impression of me.
2. Arguing over controversial issues improves my intelligence.
3. I enjoy avoiding arguments.
4. I am energetic and enthusiastic when I argue.
5. Once I finish an argument, I promise myself that I will not get into another.
6. Arguing with a person creates more problems than it solves.

7. I have a pleasant, good feeling when I win a point in an argument.
8. When I finish arguing with someone, I feel nervous and upset.
9. I enjoy a good argument over a controversial issue.
10. I get an unpleasant feeling when I realize I am about to get into an argument.
11. I enjoy defending my point of view on an issue.
12. I am happy when I keep an argument from happening.
13. I do not like to miss the opportunity to argue a controversial issue.
14. I prefer being with people who rarely disagree with me.
15. I consider an argument an exciting intellectual challenge.
16. I find myself unable to think of effective points during an argument.
17. I feel refreshed and satisfied after an argument on a controversial issue.
18. I have the ability to do well in an argument.
19. I try to avoid getting into arguments.
20. I feel excitement when I expect that a conversation I am in is leading to an argument.

Scoring:

1. Total your tendency to approach difficult conversations: 2, 4, 7, 9, 11, 13, 15, 17, 18, and 20.
2. Add 60 to the total from step 1.
3. Total your tendency to avoid difficult conversations: 1, 3, 5, 6, 8, 10, 12, 14, 16, and 19.
4. Subtract the total from step three from the total obtained in step two.

Interpretation: A score of 73–100 indicates you have a high degree of willingness to engage in arguments; a score of 56–72 indicates you have a moderate degree of willingness to engage in arguments;

LIFE-CHANGING HABIT #7: MASTERING DIFFICULT CONVERSATIONS

and scores of 20–55 indicate you have a low degree of willingness to engage arguments.

Adapted from Infante & Cancer (1982).[8]

The following are five skills to help develop your difficult conversation competence.

1. Beginning the argument with a clear proposition of fact, value, or policy to clarify where you stand relative to the different point of view.
2. Identifying and clearly articulating the problem, the cause for the problem, possible solution, and the potential good and bad consequences from the possible solution to the problem.
3. Presenting and defending your position using evidence such as specific examples and data.
4. Finding errors in judgment or reasoning in the other point of view.
5. Maintaining your relationship during the conversation by affirming points of view you can appreciate and not interrupting the other person. If the conversation becomes confrontational, it is better to stop the conversation than respond with further aggression.

How to Assess and Improve Your Upward Dissent Ability. Some of the most challenging conversations you will have are those with your leader. Not all approaches are equally effective in having these difficult conversations. The following short self-assessment can be used to quickly identify your preferred approach and assess if it is the most effective approach.

Instructions: Using the following upward dissent scale, indicate your degree of agreement with the statement in situations involving disagreements with your leader or leaders higher in the organization.

1 = strongly disagree, 2 = disagree, 3 = agree some and disagree some, 4 = agree, 5 = strongly agree.

1. I talk to someone higher up in the organization than my direct supervisor.
2. I gather evidence to support my concern.
3. I bring up my concern numerous times.
4. I say I'll quit if the organization doesn't do something about the problem.
5. I focus on the facts surrounding the issue.
6. I raise the issue repeatedly.
7. I suggest that I'm considering quitting if the organization doesn't do something.
8. I talk to an organizational officer higher in the chain of command.
9. I threaten to resign if my concerns aren't addressed.
10. I present solutions, not just problems.
11. I talk to my boss' boss.
12. I make several attempts to draw attention to the concern.
13. I use facts to support my claim.
14. I claim that the problem is serious enough to make me quit.
15. I go above my direct supervisor's head to voice my concern.
16. I continue to mention my concern until it gets addressed.
17. I go over my boss' head.
18. I repeat my concern as often as possible.
19. I threaten to quit.
20. I present a well-thought-out solution to the problem.

Scoring: Total your responses for each potential approach. The higher the score, the more likely you are to use that particular approach.

Items 2, 5, 10, 13, and 20 = Prosocial
Items 4, 7, 9, 14, and 19 = Threatening

LIFE-CHANGING HABIT #7: MASTERING DIFFICULT CONVERSATIONS

Items 1, 8, 11, 15, and 17 = Circumvention
Items 3, 6, 12, 16, and 18 = Repetition

Adapted from Passing and Kava (2013)[9]

The most effective approach is a prosocial approach, where you make a direct-factual appeal or present a solution. When you support a difficult conversation with evidence or offer a solution along with the problem, it reduces the threat to your leader. As you may have guessed, the least effective approach is threatening the leader because it does the most relational damage.

KEY POINTS—MASTERING DIFFICULT CONVERSATIONS

- Leadership is a relationship, and communication is fundamental to every conversation.
- Ultimately, the viewpoints of the leader and the follower engaged in a conversation define that conversation as difficult.
- Stress and pressure associated with these conversations make leaders vulnerable to mistakes and further amplify a conversation's difficulty.
- All leaders, at some point, wrestle with the perceived dichotomy of being a leader and being vulnerable.
- Leadership vulnerability involves the willingness to take risks that might end in failure or create the best of what might be for the work, the worker, and the workplace.
- Conflict is common in life and work. But productive conflict is rare.
- Conflict becomes worse when avoided or ignored.
- Focusing on what matters most defuses the emotional intensity of the conversation, improves effectiveness, reduces repeat discussions, and improves the leader-follower relationship.

REFLECTION QUESTIONS—MASTERING DIFFICULT CONVERSATIONS

- Think of three recent conversations where you felt vulnerable. Name the situation. What was the circumstance or trigger?
- Are you creating an environment where others can speak up without feeling embarrassed or rejected? Are followers being vulnerable with you?
- Are you having the right conversations? Consider content, pattern, and relationship.
- Is there a difficult conversation you're avoiding?
- When was the last time you disagreed with your leader? Did you take action or avoid the conflict? What can you do to improve how you handle conflict differently the next time?
- How well are you showing and telling others that you value them?
- Are you inappropriately using positional power in difficult conversations?

• • •

Endnotes

1. Brown, B. (2015). *Daring Greatly: How the Courage to Be Vulnerable Transforms the Way We Live, Love, Parent, and Lead*. Penguin Publishing Group. P.18
2. Bartell, R. (2011). *Before the call: The communication playbook*. Hudson House.
3. Hayes, J. (2008). "Workplace Conflict and How Businesses Can Harness It to Thrive" [PDF]. *CPP Global Human Capital Report*. https://www.themyersbriggs.com/-/media/f39a8b7fb4fe4daface552d9f485c825.ashx
4. Ayoko, O.B. (2016). "Workplace conflict and willingness to cooperate: The importance of apology and forgiveness." *The International Journal of Conflict Management*, 27(2), 172-198. https://doi.org/10.1108/IJCMA-12-2014-0092
5. Patterson, K., Grenny, J., McMillan, R., & Switzler, A. (2021). *Crucial Conversations: Tools for Talking When Stakes Are High* (Third ed.). McGraw Hill.

6. Brown, Brené. "The Power of Vulnerability." Filmed June 2010 in Houston, Texas. TED video 20:03, TEDxHouston.https://www.ted.com/talks/brene_brown_the_power_of_vulnerability?language=en
7. Schaubhut, N. A. (2007). Technical brief for the Thomas-Kilmann conflict mode instrument. *CPP Research Department.* https://kilmanndiagnostics.com/wp-content/uploads/2018/04/TKI_Technical_Brief.pdf
8. Infante, D.A., & Rancer, A.S. (1982). "A Conceptualization and Measure of Argumentativeness." *Journal of Personality Assessment*, 46(1), 72-80. https://doi.org/10.1207/s15327752jpa4601_13
9. Kassing, J.W., & Kava, W. (2013). "Assessing Disagreement Expressed to Management: Development of the Upward Dissent Scale." *Communication Research Reports*, 30(1), 46-56.

Life-Changing Habit #8
Being Trustworthy

"Without trust we don't truly collaborate; we merely coordinate or, at best, cooperate. It is trust that transforms a group of people into a team."
—STEPHEN M.R. COVEY[1]

OVERVIEW

Trusting relationships make big things happen for leaders. And the only way to create trusting relationships is to be trustworthy. Of course, no leader intends not to be trustworthy. However, playing it safe and trying to avoid failure does not naturally produce high-quality trust-based relationships.

Trust in leadership is becoming rarer in every organization. A recent large-scale study of trust involving twenty-eight countries and over 33,000 respondents revealed that the crisis-driven workplace is speeding up a decline in trust.[2] Trust holds organizations together, making the decline in the workplace particularly concerning in today's volatile, uncertain, complex, and ambiguous workplace. Is it is possible for leaders to build trust in a world of constant change?

Two common themes in the research on building trust are transparency and relationships. The goal for being trustworthy is to create safety by being open and candid and showing caring and respect. Creating intimacy in relationships is dependent on being personal and willing to have difficult conversations. Relationships require leaders to listen, consider, and discuss other points of view to create a shared idea of success. A "my way or the highway" leadership style does not build trust. It is essential to understand the context and perspectives of others.

During change, communication that builds trust includes a vision of the idealized goal for the organization, personal excitement, and support for followers. Trust improves the outcome of change.[3] Establishing trust during change requires executive leaders to focus intently on building rapport, inviting and responding to emotional responses, and explaining change clearly and concisely.

Defining Being Trustworthy

Trust is the currency of successful business relationships. It is a reliance on the character, capability, or truth of others. Leaders that are humble, reliable, credible, and transparent are considered trustworthy.[4] Being trustworthy brings out your best, the best in others, and the organization. Trustworthiness is earned through actions a leader takes.

VIRTUES OF BEING TRUSTWORTHY

Three practical ways (virtues) of being trustworthy are being credible, reliable, and transparent.

Being Credible

As an executive leader or business owner, it is possible to have the responsibility for leading without having a deep understanding or

LIFE-CHANGING HABIT #8: BEING TRUSTWORTHY

technical expertise for the specific work being done. In these situations, leaders may wonder: How important is credibility to leading? Power and influence increase with a leader's perceived knowledge and skill.[5] A leader's ability to influence is directly affected by follower perceptions. The more credibility, the greater the leader's influence. Credibility is primarily determined by others' beliefs about the leader's knowledge, competence, and goodwill.[6] Like many aspects of leadership, credibility is not something intrinsic to the leader but rather is something rationally or emotionally perceived by followers.

Business understanding and technical competence become more difficult to define at higher levels of management. However, knowledge and expertise are important factors of perceived credibility. There are many ways to consider business knowledge and technical competence, and there is overlap between them. For example, there is context knowledge such as the business environment, content knowledge such as facts about company operations, and subject matter expertise such as a job or functional specific areas like accounting or finance. Although leaders are not expected to be all-knowing and able to perform the tasks of every job in a company, a leader can enhance his or her perceived knowledge through training, education, and experience. A real threat for many executives is minimizing the importance of their knowledge and technical competence.

Goodwill is a leadership characteristic not often discussed. Leaders can display and create goodwill by being friendly, helpful, and cooperative. Most simply stated, by being authentically nice. Building mutual goodwill is not trying to be popular, but authentically caring for followers and the organization.

Being nice means being willing to have a difficult conversation and exit a colleague from a job where they are not the right fit. A leader can build goodwill by developing emotional intelligence, helping followers, and spending time establishing strong relationships.[7] Leaders can increase mutual goodwill with simple actions such as looking for opportunities to say thank you.

Being Reliable

Leaders typically do not get offered or keep leadership positions without being reliable. However, being reliable can be a real challenge for busy leaders. Reliability is determined by the frequency of interactions and consistency of the leader's expected behavior. Saying what you will do, following through, and being who you are influence perceptions of reliability.

A follower's perceptions of reliability increase with an increase in time spent working together. It is harder for new leaders to be perceived as reliable because there isn't much of a history for followers to draw upon. So if a new leader says one thing and does another, it has a greater impact on their perceived reliability.

Beyond explicit reliability, there is also implicit reliability. These are perceptions based on experiences such as what time the leader shows up to work, the clothes they wear, the way they greet people, and their personality. None of these are explicit statements, but their consistency aligns with the expectations of followers and increase followers' sense of a leader's reliability.

New leaders and those needing to improve follower perceptions of reliability can benefit by keeping specific commitments. In a chaotic work environment, it is tempting to be vague, but this does not help build reliability. Instead of stating, "I will follow up with you later," give followers a specific date and time and put it in your calendar. However, do not over-promise. If giving a particular date and time, make sure you set yourself up for success by factoring in a buffer for the unexpected. Apologize if you're unable to follow through. Don't wait until commitments are missed to apologize. As soon as you anticipate that a promise won't be kept, let the other person know. No excuses. Take responsibility.

Meetings can consume significant time for a leader and present a considerable opportunity to improve his or her reliability. Leaders set themselves up for success by confirming appointments before they happen. Before the meeting starts, state not just agendas, but the meeting purpose and goals. Send materials for meetings for others to review before the meeting so time is spent on discussions. Review the meeting agenda and objectives before beginning meetings to clarify expectations and create consistency. Begin on time and end on time—respect others' time in meetings.

Being Transparent

It is common for leaders to feel overwhelmed by the amount of information available. Emails, messages, and updates are received every minute of the day. It is hard to keep up in an always-on digital workplace. Worst of all, it is hard to find time to work on the projects that matter most. Too much information creates confusion, anxiety, and inefficiency in the workplace. Transparency is characterized by openness. But that doesn't mean sharing everything, rather only information that is relevant and honest.

Transparent communication is foundational for trusting leader-follower relationships. When leaders are transparent, they encourage participation and accept accountability. Participation promotes a culture where followers are empowered to take charge. Transparency also includes sharing all the information: the good, the bad, and the ugly. When leaders reveal only part of a story, they run the risk of followers feeling manipulated. Being transparent often involves sharing both the known and unknown, as well as a timeline for when information is anticipated to be shared. Beyond enhancing a leader's trustworthiness, being transparent reduces anxiety and uncertainty and fosters improved leader-follower relationships.[8] At a company level, the benefits of transparency include improved organizational performance and healthy workplace culture.

CHEERLEADER JIM

Jim was a CEO of a nonprofit volunteer organization providing critical services for a small town. Jim's team was small and had gone through significant changes over the past few years. The current team was made up of two long-time employees and a few full-time and part-time employees that were all new within the past year. The nonprofit organization constantly needed additional funding to meet the growing needs in the community.

Jim was well-liked by his team, most volunteers, and community residents. He was a great cheerleader for the community and everyone on his team. He always would see the best in people and was optimistic about the future. He was also able to find benefactors to help with the community's growing needs for additional services.

Jim was a dreamer and always wanted to do more for his community. As a result, he kept pushing his team to start new projects. Jim was not detail-oriented and relied on his team to work through the specifics to get new projects implemented.

However, if team members didn't respond quickly, he would step in and take charge of project decisions. Then, before the new service could get fully implemented, Jim already had another idea and would move on to another project. His team felt overwhelmed by the needs in the community and a lack of resources to get the new work completed without falling behind on what already was in place. Although honest and kind to a fault, he was not consistent or reliable in his approach to leadership.

Jim believed the scope of team roles was too big. In response to the community's financial support, he restructured their work and added a few new part-time positions to the team. Jim believed this would help expand the services and bring better results. Jim saw the greatest challenge facing the organization as filling open roles with qualified employees. He needed to find the right people to fill the open positions and hire for new services.

After a few months with the new structure in place, the same old issues appeared for the team again. Jim's team felt frustrated and more confused because of the added complexity of additional work and new employees. Jim didn't connect how his lack of reliability impacted the team's trust in him as a leader, its willingness to innovate, or its declining performance. He was too nice and not a leader. He left too many hard questions unanswered.

EXAMPLES OF ABSENCE OF TRUST

The bad habit of an absence of trust can be recognized by leaders that lack credibility, reliability, and transparency.

Lacking Credibility

A leader's daily actions can either create or destroy credibility. The distance from the frontline increases as a leader ascends within an organization, threatening the leader's credibility vis-a-vis the work. A common threat for leaders, especially those in executive positions, is a desire to move too quickly. When leaders make decisions without soliciting input and speak about the business from past experiences, followers feel undervalued. Also, rarely do all the variables of any job in any business stay constant year-over-year, and not listening limits true understanding.

Sadly, another avoidable mistake that damages a leader's credibility is failing to thank followers for a job well done. Too often, leaders get caught in the trap of moving from crisis to crisis without pausing to create goodwill by recognizing great work. Leaders without credibility lose their ability to persuade and influence followers beyond applying positional power. And when positional power is overused, it has many hidden costs. Leaders who lack credibility may control the work done in the short-term but will lose the commitment of followers.

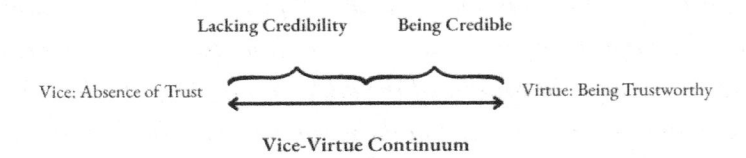

Lacking Credibility — Being Credible

Vice: Absence of Trust — Virtue: Being Trustworthy

Vice-Virtue Continuum

Example Attributes and Behaviors

LACKING CREDIBILITY	BEING CREDIBLE
• Not listening and learning • Thinking a paycheck is enough of a thank you • Being self-focused and self-supportive	• Being knowledgeable and experienced • Saying thank you • Being empathic and cooperative

Lacking Reliability

Reliability is an unwritten expectation of leaders. Leaders who say they will do something then fail to follow through or do something different are perceived to be unreliable. For example, leaders who discuss the importance of following procedures in one meeting and in the next meeting critique followers for not taking innovative approaches to solve problems are unreliable. When leaders assign tasks one day and take over the work the next day, it negatively impacts followers' perceptions of their leaders' reliability. A lack of reliability causes a range of emotions within followers, from frustration and rejection to even blatant disdain for the leader. Being unreliable damages followers' perceptions of leadership trustworthiness.

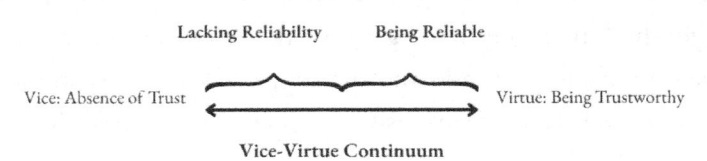

Lacking Reliability — Being Reliable

Vice: Absence of Trust — Virtue: Being Trustworthy

Vice-Virtue Continuum

LIFE-CHANGING HABIT #8: BEING TRUSTWORTHY

Example Attributes and Behaviors

LACKING RELIABILITY	BEING RELIABLE
• Poor communication and follow-through • Chasing the shiny object • Unable to say no • Unpredictable	• What is said is done • Clear priorities • Able to say no • Showing up authentically

Lacking Transparency

When leaders lack transparency, it fuels suspicion and rumors in the workplace. A lack of transparency increases misinterpretations, causing misunderstanding, distrust, and follower uncertainty and anxiety.[9] A lack of transparency can come from a leader's failure to act or, worse, their intentional actions. Failing to communicate everything needed is not uncommon for leaders pulled in multiple directions. Communicating without mistakes requires careful consideration of what to share, who needs to know, and clarifying when required. When leaders purposefully withhold information to manipulate a situation, it creates a toxic culture. At best, purposeful manipulation is irritating to others and undermines the goals and interests of the business.

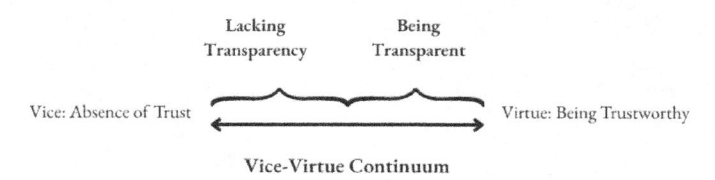

Vice: Absence of Trust ←————— Lacking Transparency | Being Transparent —————→ Virtue: Being Trustworthy

Vice-Virtue Continuum

Example Attributes and Behaviors

LACKING TRANSPARENCY	BEING TRANSPARENT
• Guarded • Dishonest or telling a "white lie" • Sharing everything • Manipulative (Machiavellian)	• Open • Honest—the good, bad, and the ugly information • Sharing timely, relevant information • Supportive

CAUSES, CONSEQUENCES & COMPLICATIONS OF ABSENCE OF TRUST

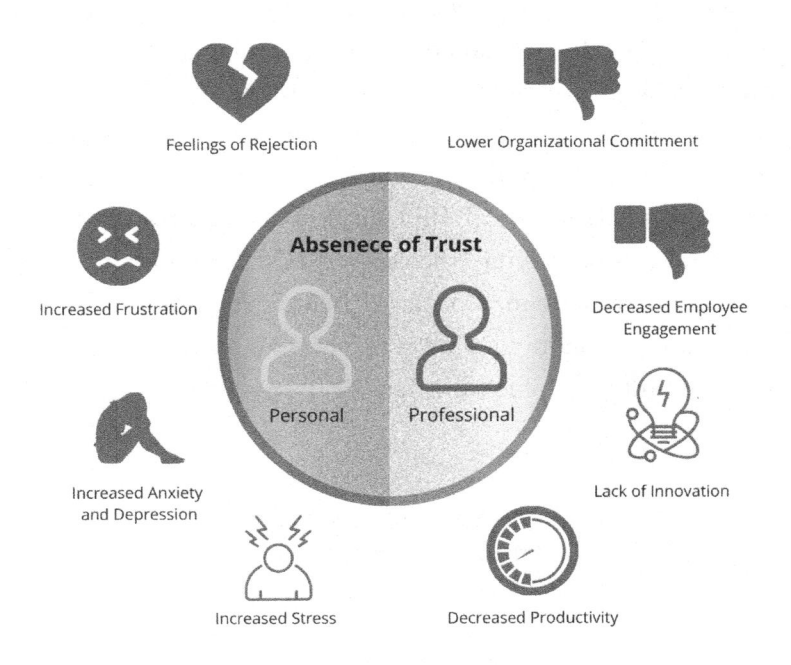

- Feelings of Rejection
- Lower Organizational Comittment
- Increased Frustration
- Absenece of Trust (Personal / Professional)
- Decreased Employee Engagement
- Increased Anxiety and Depression
- Lack of Innovation
- Increased Stress
- Decreased Productivity

An increasingly crisis-driven and complex workplace and declining trust in leaders are contributing to an absence of trust in the workplace. In a fast-changing workplace, leaders are moving quickly between positions. This limits the amount of their company-specific technical experience and threatens the perception of their leadership capability. Additionally, reliability is an increasing challenge as more followers are remote or in fractional positions, making it challenging for leaders to interact with their followers.

Employees and leaders also face a deluge of information from advances in technology. The overwhelming amount of data increases the complexity for leaders to provide only relevant information. Also, there is growing distrust in information source credibility. An absence of trust in leaders presents a unique challenge for followers who don't know where to turn to get trustworthy information.

The leader's personality and approach to leadership can cause an absence of trust. Leaders that over-rely on positional power or are manipulative lose credibility among followers. Likewise, humility moderates trust. The less humility a leader displays, the lower the trust in a relationship. Humble leaders who adopt an other-centric leadership style improve credibility and trustworthiness.

Trust is the currency of business relationships, and an absence of trust can bankrupt the organization and its employees. At an individual level, a lack of trust contributes to feelings of frustration, rejection, stress, anxiety, and depression. An absence of trust at the organizational level undermines the goals and interests of the business and the engagement and organizational commitment of employees. When leaders in an organization are unable to trust, the organization is less likely to innovate and take risks, holding back performance and productivity in the organization.

TRANSFORMATIONAL TOOLS & EXERCISES FOR BEING TRUSTWORTHY

How to Assess Your Relationship Trust. All leaders can benefit from taking stock of their relationships. Measuring your trustworthiness provides helpful, structured insights with the potential to enhance the quality of the relationship. Also, applying this approach across all your relationships can help you get a broad view, making it easier to identify trends and potential development opportunities across all your relationships.

Instructions: Identify a leader-follower relationship you want to measure. Then, reflecting on the past few months, assign a rating for each credibility, reliability, and intimacy attribute of your actions. You may want to reflect on the discussion of these attributes earlier in this chapter. Also, choose the answer that seems the most generally true for you; don't search for exceptions to the rule or focus on one specific aspect of your leadership. 1 = almost never true, 2 = rarely true, 3 = occasionally true, 4 = often true, 5 = almost always true.

How to Communicate with Trust. The leading global coaching community for advancing professional and personal development is the International Coaching Federation (ICF). According to the ICF, the following six behaviors are specific, practical ways leaders can build trust-based relationships:[10]

1. Shows genuine concern for clients' welfare and future
2. Continuously demonstrates personal integrity, honesty, and sincerity
3. Establishes clear agreements and keeps promises
4. Demonstrates respect for clients' perceptions, learning style, and personal being
5. Provides ongoing support for and champions new behaviors and actions, including those involving risk-taking and fear of failure
6. Asks permission to coach clients in new, sensitive areas

How to Assess Work Styles and Quickly Build Trustworthiness. An excellent way for new leaders and teams to ramp up getting to know

LIFE-CHANGING HABIT #8: BEING TRUSTWORTHY

each other and trustworthiness is through a work-style assessment. Assessments help leaders and followers identify and discuss how their work styles impact relationships, communication, and productivity. In a group with a qualified trainer, assessments create a safe environment for leaders and followers to explore differences. The enhanced transparency revealed through the assessment equips leaders to approach relationships to meet unique needs. There are numerous work-style assessments, including the DISC temperament instrument. In addition to individual reports, the tool provides a good structure for leaders and followers to explore and identify strategies to transform personal and team relationships. For more information regarding the DISC assessment, please go to www.everthingdisc.com.

How to Increase Transparency. A fun and creative way to enhance trustworthiness in a new relationship is to use a life map exercise as an introduction. I first encountered this exercise when I met a colleague from Italy. As a typical U.S. employee, when meeting my colleague for the first time, I focused on the task at hand. However, my colleague used this tool to help us get to know each other and support our working relationship.

Life maps can be as creative and revealing as the leader would like. The maps are visual timelines using pictures, personal quotes, hobbies, interests, and anything else that helps the leader safely demonstrate transparency and credibility. This allows the leader to learn what is essential in a safe way.

KEY POINTS—BEING TRUSTWORTHY

- Trusting relationships make big things happen for leaders.
- A "your way or the highway" leadership style does not build trust in relationships.
- Relationships require leaders to listen, consider, and discuss other points of view to create a shared idea of success.
- Trustworthy leaders are humble, reliable, credible, and transparent.

- Being considered a trustworthy leader must be earned.
- Credibility is primarily determined by the beliefs about the leader's knowledge, competence, and goodwill.
- Power and influence increase with a leader's perceived ability to possess and display knowledge and skill.
- Leaders display and create goodwill by being friendly, helpful, and cooperative, i.e., being authentically nice.
- Reliability is based on the frequency of interactions and consistency of the leader's expected behavior.
- Beyond the perceptions of explicit reliability, there is also implicit reliability. These are perceptions based on experiences such as what time the leader shows up to work, the clothes they wear, the way they greet people, and their personality.
- Transparency is characterized by openness. But that doesn't mean sharing everything, rather only information that is relevant and honest.
- When leaders reveal only one side of a story, they run the risk of followers feeling manipulated.

REFLECTION QUESTIONS—BEING TRUSTWORTHY

- Do you inherently trust or distrust others? What makes someone trustworthy to you?
- How would you rate yourself on a scale of 1–10, with one being very low and ten being very high on the aspects of transparency, reliability, and credibility?
- Considering your most important relationships, force rank them from top to bottom based on trust. What are the similarities and differences between those at the top and those at the bottom? What is needed to improve trust in the relationships at the bottom?
- Consider a relationship where you have lost trust. What specific behaviors did they have or not have that led to the loss of your

trust? How would you rate them on transparency, reliability, and credibility?
- When trust is broken in a relationship, can it be repaired? How might you be a part of the change to repair the trust?
- How important is being able to trust your leader and those you work with?
- How do your individual differences influence your approach to building trust-based relationships with others?
- Does humility influence trustworthiness?

• • •

Endnotes

1. Covey, S., & Merrill, R. (2006). *The Speed of Trust: The One Thing That Changes Everything*. Free Press.
2. Ries, T.E. (2021). "21st Annual Edelman Trust Barometer" [PDF]. *Edelman*. https://www.edelman.com/sites/g/files/aatuss191/files/2021-01/2021-edelman-trust-barometer.pdf
3. Men, L.R., Yue, C.A., & Liu, Y. (2020). "Vision, passion, and care:" The impact of charismatic executive leadership communication on employee trust and support for organizational change. *Public Relations Review, 46*(3).
4. Maister, D.H., Green, C.H., & Galford, R.M. (2000). *The Trusted Advisor*. Free Press.
5. Yukl, G. (2012.) *Leadership In Organizations* (8th ed.).
6. Hovland, C., Janis, I., & Kelley, H. (1953). *Communication and Persuasion: Psychological Studies of Opinion Change*. Yale University Press.
7. Cameron, K. (2012). *Positive Leadership: Strategies for Extraordinary Performance*. Berrett-Koehler Publishers.
8. Yue, C., Men, L., & Ferguson, M. (2019). "Bridging transformational leadership, transparent communication, and employee openness to change: The mediating role of trust." *Public Relations Review, 45*(3), 101779. https://doi.org/10.1016/j.pubrev.2019.04.012
9. Men, R.L. & Bowen, S.A. (2016). *Excellence in Internal Communication Management*. Business Expert Press.
10. International Coach Federation (ICF). (2019). Updated ICF core competencies. https://coachingfederation.org/app/uploads/2021/03/ICF-Core-Competencies-updated.pdf

Life-Changing Habit #9
Embracing Failure

> "Success consists of going from failure to
> failure without loss of enthusiasm."
> —WINSTON CHURCHILL[1]

OVERVIEW

Being a leader is as exciting as it is challenging. There are always new opportunities that give a greater sense of purpose and opportunities to learn and create. However, there are also many challenges with consequences that scale to leadership responsibility.

Every leader fails at some point in work or life. Although significant investments and emphasis are placed on preventing failures by leaders and employees, they still happen. It's not hard to find examples of failure. Many well-known brands have been negatively impacted by public failures to maintain quality, behave ethically, or respond in a socially responsible way.

The word "failure" has different meanings to different people at different times. Finishing a marathon by walking past the finish line can be viewed both as a failure and success. What constitutes a failure is not always clear and is usually personal. According to the Merriam-Webster dictionary, failure is *a lack of success*. It is a lack of success in some effort or a situation in which something does not work as expected. It is logical to make the leap using this definition that the last thing a leader should do is embrace failure.

However, failure is not always bad, but a fear of failure puts results at risk. Fear minimizes experimentation and risk-taking, which impact innovation and change. Leaders should support the pursuit of small-scale experiments to track and celebrate small wins as well as being open to interesting failures that create a learning environment toward meaningful progress.[2] Also, if leaders adopt an orientation where employee outcomes are connected to the company's success, then feedback loops will promote learning from failure.[3] A leader's perception, and their response to failure, determine what defines success in any given situation.

Business owners and leaders are often considered resilient, but if honest, they also experience fear of failure. Is it possible for leaders to embrace failure as a means of increasing innovation in the workplace? Embracing failure enables leaders to champion and support risky behaviors and actions that lead to personal and professional improvement. Without some level of risk, there can be no reward. Although there are many ways to fail, there are also many ways to succeed.

Defining Embracing Failure

Leaders and organizations are not paid to fail. Still, leaders and organizations that stay the same fail to get ahead. Successful leaders and organizations fail more than they succeed.[4] Embracing failure as a natural part of learning is fundamental for leaders and organizations to grow and succeed, but this is challenging to grasp. Leaders who embrace failure are vulnerable, adopt a mindset that failure is the beginning of something great, and shape the culture to support excusable interesting failure.

LIFE-CHANGING HABIT #9: EMBRACING FAILURE

VIRTUES OF EMBRACING FAILURE

Two practical ways (virtues) to embrace failure are having a learning mindset and supporting failure.

Learning Mindset

The difficult first step to the leadership habit of embracing failure is reframing failure as learning. Attitudes influence behaviors. Until failure is perceived more broadly than a lack of success, attitudes will remain that failure should be avoided. A learning mindset enables followers and cultures to value failure as an essential step in the learning process. However, a learning mindset is rare in the workplace, but not because of a lack of desire to learn and grow. No organization is looking to stay the same. The widely held point of view is that the risk of failure outweighs the perceived uncertain benefits of learning.

Leaders make thousands of decisions each day. Research has identified that our brain uses shortcuts, which the field of psychology labels biases. A bias is a predisposition. One commonly held bias is toward safety. Simply stated, many leaders tend to want to avoid losses to a greater extent than they wish to achieve gains. In other words, leaders would rather avoid losing money than take risks to make money. Safety bias influences risk and failure avoidance.

The higher the fear of failure, the more likely an individual or organization will avoid taking necessary risks. Leaders that redefine the concept of failure as learning in the workplace unlock significant benefits. A learning mindset increases levels of engagement, seeking feedback and challenges, persistence, productivity, and well-being.[5] A learning mindset helps leaders and organizations grow beyond challenges.

A few proven steps leaders can take to shift attitudes toward failure and influence a learning mindset in the workplace follow.

- **Architecting culture.** The artifacts, espoused values, and basic assumptions of leaders influence the culture of the organization. Are the things that are seen, felt, or heard in the workplace supportive of a learning mindset? Do leaders speak supportively of a learning mindset during a crisis? Do the things taken for granted within the company support a learning mindset?
- **Coaching.** An effective executive coach can challenge false assumptions and encourage, stretch, and challenge motivations to avoid failure at work.
- **Learning goals.** Goals that focus on the desire to improve versus to achieve performance outcomes cultivate the right mindset. A learning goal orientation mindset is essential.

Supporting Failure

Failing to change leads to business failure, and an unhealthy fear of failure is a threat to success. Fear can dominate choices and limit experimentation required for growth and innovation. The fear of failure is proven to trigger psychological reactions that keep leaders from taking risks to exploit existing opportunities or pursue new opportunities.[6] But can leaders support failure and be successful?

Leaders and organizations that are not improving are falling behind. It is easy to rationalize that unless leaders and organizations are willing to take risks and accept failure as learning, they won't grow. But no one enjoys failing. Also, in an increasingly competitive global marketplace, failing can threaten an organization's survival and have severe consequences for the leader's career. Without leaders being intentional about reinforcing a learning mindset and supporting failure, it is unlikely that followers will overcome a fear of failure.

Leaders who are supportive of failure are vulnerable and able to differentiate between excusable and inexcusable failures. Leaders who embrace failure are transparent about their failures and don't blame

LIFE-CHANGING HABIT #9: EMBRACING FAILURE

others when they occur. In addition to being transparent, they are also good active listeners. When leaders practice vulnerability, it creates a safe environment where followers are more willing to be open with failures.

It is fairly easy to differentiate between achieving a goal or missing a goal. However, embracing failure requires the leader to have a keen awareness and the ability to differentiate between excusable mistakes and those that are the result of carelessness.[7] This differentiation enables leaders to equally reward interesting failures and to achieve goals. Positive risk-taking behaviors need to be rewarded and recognized even when they do not directly result in achieving the desired goal. Leaders are rewarding risk avoidance when they punish well-thought-out and executed plans that result in interesting failure.[8]

Supporting failure does not imply that leaders ignore the fear of failure. Instead, they recognize the negative influence of fear and use it as an advantage. Leaders who are supportive of failure create a collaborative environment where risks can be analyzed and good ideas utilized, no matter where the idea originates. This collaboration builds confidence and courage in followers to express thoughts and take risks. The goal of leaders that embrace failure is to encourage a learning mindset and empower risk-taking behaviors to achieve personal and professional success and significance.

Followers quickly form opinions about leaders. A servant leadership style is aligned with the attitudes and actions required for supporting failure. For example, the servant leadership attribute of humility encourages vulnerability and openness with failures. Also, the attribute of selfless love overcomes the influences of emotions associated with failure.[9] Leaders who consistently apply servant leadership create benefits beyond supporting failure.

SARAH'S COSTLY LESSON

Sarah was the senior director of Human Resources for U.S. operations within a multibillion-dollar global manufacturing organization. She joined the firm three years earlier. Within two years she was promoted to her current role as a part of the global HR leadership team.

The HR function within the company was primarily to administer benefits and provide policies to keep the organization out of trouble. However, Sarah had visions of utilizing the scale of the organization and leveraging best practices to advance the HR function to be more strategic. Sarah loved HR, the company's mission, and was committed to her work. Her passion came through in conversations, and she was driven to get results. She always believed things could be better.

When Sarah started her new role, she was assigned Don as a mentor. He was a seasoned HR leader. Don warned Sarah to take her time getting to know the business. He shared that the organization was comfortable with how things were done and didn't do change well. Sarah was conflicted because she saw plenty of opportunities to improve processes but knew she didn't have all the information to make the best decisions. She was torn between moving fast to add value for employees and being correct.

After a few months into her new role, Sarah was approached by a leader within operations. He had an idea to revise the performance management processes to better align with the organization's new strategies. He believed that the current performance management system did not equally support all of the different business areas.

Sarah wanted to understand the needs of the frontline employees better. She had this on her list of things to do, but now she had a partner in need of help. Sarah moved ahead, getting buy-in from different parts of the business on the need for change.

Unfortunately, the company's new strategies did not deliver the results, and revenue was declining. Business leaders began to push back on the training and expense with the new performance management system needed to effectively manage the process. Sarah's

LIFE-CHANGING HABIT #9: EMBRACING FAILURE

leader encouraged her to move ahead, given the investment already made and business needs.

Sarah's team implemented the new process aligned with HR best practices. The team conducted training sessions, but the organization felt stretched too thin to participate. Sarah felt stuck and doomed to fail. She approached her leader and reviewed her plans, and together they decided to continue.

The implementation was completed as scheduled. But the after-action review revealed that the results were not what Sarah or anyone else had hoped. Leaders felt the training distracted their teams and contributed to the quarter's losses. The additional operating costs from the new system definitely didn't help. Sarah also realized her new team had identified these concerns earlier but neglected to bring them to her attention.

Sarah failed to consider the cultural influence and had minimized concerns of timing. There was a prevailing belief in the company that you just figure out how to make things work, and failure to execute on an executive leader's idea was not an option. Sarah's passion for improving and her limited time in the new position kept the team from being vulnerable and open with their concerns.

Sarah's leader took responsibility for moving forward and considered it an excusable failure. However, frontline leaders and Sarah's peers viewed her and the HR team as out of touch and not understanding the business. The rapid changes implemented after Sarah's arrival and the emphasis on best practices from outside the company were ultimately rejected. She worked to change those perceptions over the next few years with limited success.

EXAMPLES OF FEAR OF FAILURE

The bad habit of a fear of failure can be recognized by leaders who have a fixed mindset in order to avoid failure.

Fixed Mindset

A fixed mindset views work from a performance orientation. Failure is considered avoidable, as is anything less than meeting expectations. The threats associated with maintaining the status quo are viewed as better than the risks of failing while trying to improve. Leaders place a premium on avoiding failure when making decisions. Businesses need to achieve their goals to succeed. However, a fixed mindset leads to a culture that fears innovation.

Leaders with a fixed mindset have a high degree of fear associated with failing. They will avoid collaboration because mistakes are viewed as the leader being incompetent. Leaders with a fixed mindset are likely to avoid stretch assignments or retreat at the first sign of missing expectations.

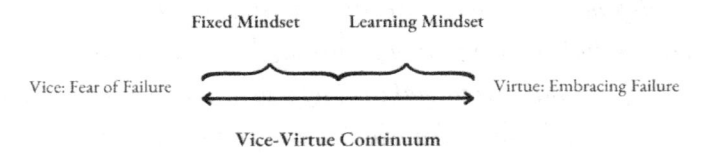

Vice: Fear of Failure ←——— Fixed Mindset | Learning Mindset ———→ Virtue: Embracing Failure

Vice-Virtue Continuum

Example Attributes and Behaviors

FIXED MINDSET	LEARNING MINDSET
• Failure as avoidable	• Failure as necessary
• Performance goal orientation	• Learning goal orientation
• High fear of failure	• Low fear of failure
• Risk averse	• Risk tolerant

Avoiding Failure

No one wants to fail. But avoiding failure in the workplace can lead to valuing continuous improvements over innovation. While this approach can lead to high-quality and low-cost products and services,

LIFE-CHANGING HABIT #9: EMBRACING FAILURE

the hidden financial and non-financial costs of avoiding failure are severe. In organizations that avoid failure, leaders are guarded about errors. When confronted, they tend to shift blame rather than accept responsibility. Failure is punished. Beyond the obvious organizational threat to innovation, leaders experience increased levels of anxiety as the fear of failing increases. A failure to learn and grow leads to repeat errors and costly avoidable mistakes in the workplace. Failure allows the leader to reconsider the task and envision a more successful outcome.

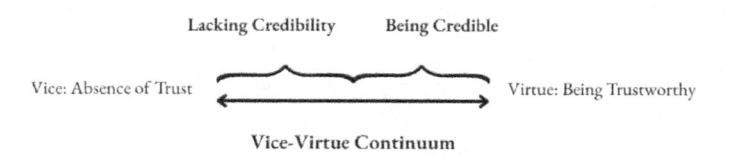

Lacking Credibility   Being Credible

Vice: Absence of Trust   Virtue: Being Trustworthy

Vice-Virtue Continuum

Example Attributes and Behaviors

AVOIDING FAILURE	SUPPORTING FAILURE
• Transfer blame	• Responsible humility
• Guarded about failure	• Vulnerable and transparent about failure
• Differentiates between success and failure	• Differentiates between excusable and inexcusable failure
• Individual ideation	• Collaborative ideation

CAUSES, CONSEQUENCES & COMPLICATIONS OF FEAR OF FAILURE

Diagram: Fear of Failure (Personal / Professional) with surrounding factors: Avoidance, Repeatable Errors, Powerlessness, Decreased Experimentation, Anxiety, Lack of Innovation, Helplessness, Risk Avoiidance

The fear of failing can be a rational and irrational response to a real or perceived consequence of a leader's actions. Without a rational fear of failing, leaders lack the desire to evaluate the potential pros and cons associated with a new idea. A healthy fear of failure improves a leader's success. An irrational and persistent fear of failing is referred to as *atychiphobia*. This irrational fear of failure can range from mild to all-consuming in daily life. Individuals who also struggle with perfectionism can struggle with atychiphobia.

Fear of failure is characterized by feelings of embarrassment, a perceived threat to a leader's value, future uncertainty, or others' perceptions of the leader. The fear of failure causes feelings of anxiety, avoidance, loss of control, helplessness, and powerlessness at a personal level. Leaders with a dominant fear of failure avoid opportunities to develop and grow.

LIFE-CHANGING HABIT #9: EMBRACING FAILURE

At an organizational level, the complications that arise from this culture are an increase in repeatable errors and lack of necessary experimentation and risk-taking necessary for innovation. Businesses that do not innovate and change fall behind and ultimately fail.

TRANSFORMATIONAL TOOLS & EXERCISES FOR EMBRACING FAILURE

How to Measure Your Fear of Failure: Using a measurement tool to better understand your fear of failure can help you create more meaningful development plans. Fear of failure can stem from embarrassment, a threat to perceived value or future uncertainty, as well as other perceptions. The following short self-assessment can be used to quickly identify your underlying fears and benchmark with others.

Instructions: Using the following response scale, indicate your degree of agreement: -2 = Do not believe at all, -1 = Rarely believe, 0 = Believe 50% of the time, 1= Believe most of the time, 2 = Believe 100% of the time.

- When I am failing, I am afraid that I might not have enough talent.
- When I am failing, it upsets my "plan" for the future.
- When I am not succeeding, people are less interested in me.
- When I am failing, important others are disappointed.
- When I am failing, I worry about what others think about me.

Scoring: Use the following equation to determine your fear of failure score.

(Item 1 + Item 2 + Item 3 + Item 4 + Item 5) / 5 = Fear of Failure Score

The higher the score, the greater the fear of failure. The following normative scores allow you to benchmark your score.

- Scores above 1.0 are far above average.
- Scores in the range of 0.2 and -0.2 are average.
- Scores below -1.0 are far below average.

Adapted from Conroy and Metzler (2003)[10] Performance Appraisal Inventory.

How to Overcome a Fear of Failure. Targeted learning and development interventions can help leaders overcome a persistent fear of failure. Two proven approaches that can be helpful are game theory and mindfulness training.

- **Game Theory.** An environment free of potentially harmful consequences allows leaders to practice overcoming their fear of failure. There are many approaches to how game theory can be used. One practical approach is using action learning teams assigned a business challenge like expanding into a new market. Teams are set up to compete for a group of fictitious investors of leaders and internal and external subject matter experts. Teams are given time to develop an approach that will be scored using financial and non-financial measures such as culture and strategy alignment. The game environment uses real-life challenges to allow leaders to experience the emotions leaders face in their work environment without the potential risks.
- **Mindfulness.** Meditation enables leaders to focus on purpose in the moment and without judgment. It generally involves guided deep breathing and awareness of body and mind. All you need to get started is a guide, a comfortable place to sit, and three to five minutes. Several apps and free YouTube videos are available to serve as your guide.

How to Encourage Collaboration to Overcome a Fear of Failure. Collaboration is a proven process for increasing courage to overcome

LIFE-CHANGING HABIT #9: EMBRACING FAILURE

the fear of failure and enhance the quality of ideas. In today's fast-paced digital hybrid workplace, it is helpful to establish regular sessions specifically for collaboration. To effectively support the process and not have these sessions turn into more aimless reoccurring meetings, you need to provide structure.

- Sessions should have a focal point of a specific challenge or opportunity to explore. Make sure the gap between the current and the desired future is clear. Where possible, include measures that quantify the gap.
- Clarify the expectations for the meeting. Consider the who, what, when, where, and why.
- Carefully select who and how many participants will be involved. Typically, groups of five to ten with cross-functional experience are best for participant engagement.
- Send participants the problem statement you prepared in advance of the meeting.
- Consider how long you will need for the meeting. Typically, you don't want these to run more than an hour to keep everyone engaged and focused.
- Provide an opportunity for participants to engage physically, verbally, and visually, providing the group with the opportunity to participate in direct observation of the challenge.
- Encourage free-flowing, spontaneous, nonlinear divergent thinking such that many different ideas emerge.
- Confirm ground rules. Allow everyone to provide input without being judged.

KEY POINTS—EMBRACING FAILURE

- Every leader fails at some point.
- Fear of failure puts individuals and organizational results at risk. Fear minimizes experimentation and risk-taking, which are requirements for innovation and change.
- In pursuit of extraordinary things, it is best for leaders to support the pursuit of small-scale experiments to track, generate, and celebrate the small wins that create a learning environment toward meaningful progress.
- Embracing failure as a natural part of learning is fundamental for leaders and organizations to grow and succeed but challenging to grasp.
- Leaders who embrace failure are vulnerable, adopt a mindset that failure is the beginning of something great, and shape the organizational culture to be supportive of interesting failure.
- Leaders tend to want to avoid losses to a greater extent than to achieve gains.
- Leaders that redefine the relationship of failure to learning in the workplace unlock significant benefits.
- Leaders who support failure are transparent about their failures and take responsibility when they occur.
- Supporting failure requires keen awareness and the ability to differentiate between excusable mistakes and those that are the result of carelessness.
- Supporting failure does not imply that leaders ignore the fear of failure. Instead, they recognize the negative influence of fear and use it as an advantage.

LIFE-CHANGING HABIT #9: EMBRACING FAILURE

REFLECTION QUESTIONS—EMBRACING FAILURE

- What are you most proud of trying in the past three months?
- Do you tend to try new things only if you believe you can succeed? Are you taking enough risks?
- Do you consider failure shameful or a part of the process of learning?
- What is something in life or at work that you are not trying that you should? What can you lose if you don't try? What can you gain and learn if you try? How will you recover if you fail?
- What was the most recent experience where you did not meet your goal? Did you approach the situation conscientiously or carelessly? What were some of your most exciting discoveries about the project, yourself, and others? How has this shaped future decisions or actions?
- What is an area of work or life where you keep making the same mistakes?
- What opportunities do you have to improve how you collaborate with others on new ideas?

• • •

Endnotes
1. Langworth, R.M. Ed. (2011). *Churchill by Himself: The Definitive Collection of Quotations.* PublicAffairs.
2. Kouzes, J.M., & Posner, B.Z. (2017). *The Leadership Challenge* (Sixth ed.). Jossey-Bass.
3. Luhn, A. (2016). "The Learning Organization." *Creative and Knowledge Society*, 6(1), 1-13. doi:10.1515/cks-2016-0005
4. Serrat, O. (2017). "Knowledge Solutions: Tools, Methods, and Approaches to Drive Organizational Performance." *Springer Open.* https://doi.org/10.1007/978-981-10-0983-9
5. Noskeau, R., Santos, A., & Wang, W. (2021). "Connecting the Dots Between Mindset and Impostor Phenomenon, via Fear of Failure and

Goal Orientation, in Working Adults." *Frontiers in Psychology*, 12, 588438-588438. https://doi.org/10.3389/fpsyg.2021.588438

6. Kollmann, T., Stöckmann, C., & Kensbock, J. (2017). "Fear of failure as a mediator of the relationship between obstacles and nascent entrepreneurial activity—An experimental approach." *Journal of Business Venturing*, 32(3), 280-301. https://doi.org/10.1016/j.jbusvent.2017.02.002

7. Farson, R., & Keyes, R. (2002). "The Failure-Tolerant Leader." *Harvard Business Review*, 80(8), 64-148.

8. Berkun, S. (2010). *The Myths of Innovation.* O'Reilly Media, Inc.

9. Fry, L. (2003). "Toward a Theory of Spiritual Leadership." *The Leadership Quarterly*, 14(6), 693-727. doi:10.1016/j.leaqua.2003.09.001

10. Conroy, D., Metzler, J., & Hofer, S. (2003). "Factorial Invariance and Latent Mean Stability of Performance Failure Appraisals." *Structural Equation Modeling*, 10(3), 401-422.

Life-Changing Habit #10
Thinking Strategically

"Leadership is the capacity to translate vision into reality."
—WILLIAM BENNIS[1]

OVERVIEW

Nothing in the workplace is certain. No rational person would argue that the modern workplace is predictable. Leaders are forced to respond to disruptive change and ambiguity in the marketplace. Leaders create influence through shared understanding and organizational alignment. Organizations create value by capitalizing on individual actions toward worthy goals. However, organizations also desperately need leaders to adopt an approach to strategic thinking that accounts for the volatility and uncertainty in the marketplace.

Although essential, hope is not a strategy, and expecting leaders to predict the future is unrealistic. Realized strategies result from both plans created and the unpredictable realities during implementation. Strategic thinking needs to be continuous, adapting to the shifting market and organizational capability. Being successful and adaptive with strategic thinking requires leaders to think creatively and practically about the future. Leaders must be able to simplify the vision and be open to the variety of possibilities beyond the status quo.

Many organizations have a misconception that strategy is best created by executives and implemented by employees through strategic plans. Leaders need to shift from "authors" to "editors" of strategy. Followers must be motivated for businesses to succeed and achieve meaningful results. Companies are only as good as their employees. Building employee understanding of strategy is complex and essential in a fast-paced digital workplace. It is dangerous when employees don't understand the why behind the work. Leaders who can win the hearts and minds of employees create a competitive advantage.

Defining Strategic Thinking

Strategic thinking instills a sense of confidence during chaotic times. Without a well-defined strategy, it is difficult for followers to navigate conflicts and confusion created from disruptive change and ambiguity. A business strategy aligns individuals and teams toward achieving a common purpose from vision. The best strategies are developed inclusive of followers, focus on helping others for a greater good, account for mixed future realities, and are implemented. Strategic thinking involves five leadership competencies often underdeveloped:[2]

- Scanning. Awareness of weak signals that may not have any immediate bearing on the business but may be future-relevant.
- Visioning. Clarifying the organization's shared vision and dreams that benefit everyone.
- Reframing. Challenging current assumptions and fresh thinking about future possibilities and potential changes.
- Making common sense. Using an intellectual process of actively and skillfully conceptualizing, applying, analyzing, synthesizing, and evaluating data.

- Systems thinking. Investigating how different parts interrelate and contribute to specific potential outcomes.

Deliberate practice and coaching feedback help leaders shape strategic thinking habits that go beyond having motivation and commitment.

VIRTUES OF THINKING STRATEGICALLY

Two practical ways (virtues) to think strategically are being farsighted, and inclusive strategic thinking.

Being Farsighted

Strategic planning that changes dates on strategies in progress or adds new strategies in place of those completed makes no sense. A failure to consider future changes can create a negative impact. Leaders do not have to accept gambling with the company's future or rely only on reactionary planning approaches in a crisis-driven world. Leaders that are future-ready can avoid costly mistakes by seeing what could be, instead of constantly reacting at the last minute. There is a better approach to strategic planning.

Being farsighted utilizes practices from the field of strategic foresight. Strategic foresight involves looking beyond current experiences and scanning the horizon. This helps leaders identify signs of emerging trends in the margins to prepare for the future. Strategic foresight is a way of thinking critically, engaging, discovering, and acting.

Strategic foresight aims not to predict the future, but to enable better decision-making and preparedness. It is a systemic view of change, considering the likely and possible realities. Strategic foresight is intended to help leaders and organizations move from old beliefs to new possibilities. Traditional strategic planning is heavily focused on the internal organization. On the other hand, strategic foresight links the organization to the external environment, recognizing the company will operate within a larger world rather than be the only change in the world.

There are many additional benefits to leaders being farsighted beyond avoiding obsolescence. Organizations benefit from being better prepared and having the right tools and resources at the right time. Better preparation results in improved decision-making. When leaders extend the organization's focal length, it enhances change management. Most organizations do not possess the change agility to implement changes fast enough to avoid becoming obsolete. Farsighted leaders can position organizations to move from responding to creating trends to being the first to market. Leading new trends fuels revenue growth.

Inclusive Strategic Thinking

Great leaders have dreams for a better future—from sustainability to growing organizational talent, increasing organizational speed, and operating with greater purpose. To turn those dreams into workplace realities, leaders set strategies. Unfortunately, most organizations keep their strategies a secret. On average, 95 percent of employees don't know or understand their organization's strategies.[3] Is being more inclusive in the workplace a bad idea, and how inclusive should leadership be with strategic thinking?

Leveraging diversity enhances strategic thinking, creativity, engagement, and strategy quality. Although including every possible stakeholder is challenging—and questionably feasible—there is value in this concept. There is a correlation between involvement in strategy development and individual commitment to the strategy.[4] Inclusive strategic thinking benefits leaders, teams, and the bottom line.

When leaders solicit ideas from followers outside the traditionally involved management team, it improves the creativity of the ideas and reinforces that leader's value to employees. Creative ideas reflective of the customers' stated and unstated needs come from those closest to the

LIFE-CHANGING HABIT #10: THINKING STRATEGICALLY

customer and with no stake in the status quo. Also, being transparent with strategic input and processes enhances strategic outputs. When the employees responsible for implementing strategic plans are the same employees contributing to the plan, there is increased awareness, engagement, buy-in, and organizational performance.[5]

Advances in technology enable a more inclusive, timely, and less costly approach to strategic planning.[6] However, an inclusive approach has some potential challenges to address, such as bias, agility, and communication effectiveness.

- **Bias.** When being inclusive, leaders must avoid potential bias toward certain stakeholder groups. There is no need to work to be inclusive, only to then devalue input based on a bias toward received feedback. Approaches that promote anonymity of feedback have been demonstrated to reduce bias and positively impact output buy-in.
- **Agility.** Leaders need to pay attention to time and effort when being inclusive. Solid project management can help leaders avoid the trap of over-analysis.
- **Communication effectiveness.** Thoughtfully choosing the appropriate technology has many positive results. Different communication mediums have varying degrees of effectiveness with supporting in-the-moment feedback, information sharing, communication cues, emotions, and message customization. Face-to-face communication is proven to be the most effective type of communication.

KEIRA'S STRATEGIC MISCALCULATION

A significant announcement was made that sent reverberations through the entire extended leadership team on the call. The silence was deafening. Typically a light-hearted group, there were no fun conversations. Keira just announced that the organization would be focusing on increasing the business speed to disrupt the industry within the next four weeks.

Keira was the president of a small business with over one hundred employees and a double-digit revenue growth history. The company's market share had been growing, despite large competitors entering the market. This year, Keira and Christine, the leadership team responsible for the company's strategy, had decided that now was the time for a dramatic change of pace.

At best, the company was projected to grow just 2 percent this year. The pressure Keira placed on herself and the questions from the board of directors were taking a toll. She was struggling and had experienced a noticeable weight gain. Keira always wanted to present a very positive image, but it was more difficult this year than in the past.

Keira noticed the silence on the call with her extended leadership team and ended the call by mentioning that she would be holding meetings with each individual team to discuss what increasing the business speed would mean for each one and why it was necessary. A few on the call commented that they appreciated her openness and willingness to listen.

Keira held the meetings, but the response from the teams was that her ideas would be impractical within the suggested time frame. A few argued the change would disrupt their company as much as did the competition. Some suggested her proposals seemed a better fit for sales than collaboration.

Keira was frustrated by the negative feedback. It confirmed her suspicions that the team had become change-resistant, making the point for the new idea.

The meetings were a disaster. Keira agreed to push back the timeline to the end of the summer, giving the team additional time—yet still much less than requested. The group felt devalued due to having their input ignored. The team could not meet the second deadline set by Keira, and achieved about 75 percent of Keira's strategy.

Keira's desire to move quickly and her belief that she had the best view of the strategies needed led to significant gaps. Both leadership team engagement and execution speed suffered.

Exclusive strategic thinking not only impacts the quality of the strategies designed but comes with hidden employee costs.

EXAMPLES OF LACK OF STRATEGIC THINKING

The bad habit of a lack of strategic planning can be recognized by leaders being near-sighted and exclusive with strategic thinking.

Being Nearsighted

"No one saw it coming" is a common phrase to describe a nearsighted leader. Not being prepared is stressful and costly. Market myopia is the business term for lack of ability to see the bigger picture. Leaders with a nearsighted focal length are caught up in winning the day, which is both essential and immediately rewarding. However, losing sight of the big picture leaves leaders and organizations constantly reacting and unable to capitalize on the benefits of evolving trends. Developing winning strategies requires leaders to manage future uncertainty.

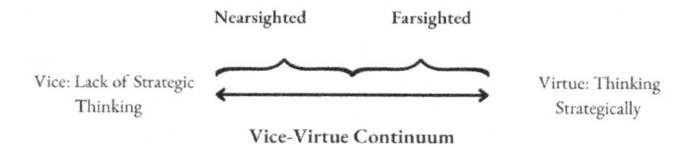

	Nearsighted	Farsighted	
Vice: Lack of Strategic Thinking	←	→	Virtue: Thinking Strategically

Vice-Virtue Continuum

Example Attributes and Behaviors

BEING NEARSIGHTED	BEING FARSIGHTED
• Focus on the day	• Able to see the big picture
• Sees only what is	• Sees what is and what could be
• Relies on hope for the future	• Prepares for the future
• Responding and reacting	• Creating trends

Exclusive Strategic Thinking

Leaders face a seemingly endless number of demands on their time. Top-down strategic thinking can appear to be a reasonable solution. Also, engaging others in strategic thinking takes courage. The bad habit of exclusive strategic thinking is easy to justify, especially when those closest to the frontline don't have the time or desire to be involved. Often, there are numerous legitimate excuses for leaders being exclusive vis-a-vis strategic thinking. However, this bad habit leads to an unnecessary barrier between planners and doers. In addition to the apparent threats, such as a lack of strategic buy-in, confusion, and engagement, there is the potential to reinforce a toxic culture—one with a shared belief among strategic planners that the input from certain groups or levels of employees is better than input from others.

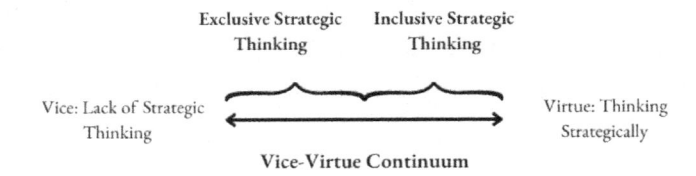

Vice: Lack of Strategic Thinking — Exclusive Strategic Thinking | Inclusive Strategic Thinking — Virtue: Thinking Strategically

Vice-Virtue Continuum

LIFE-CHANGING HABIT #10: THINKING STRATEGICALLY

Example Attributes and Behaviors

EXCLUSIVE STRATEGIC THINKING	INCLUSIVE STRATEGIC THINKING
• A barrier between planners and doers • Looking for confirmation • Top-down without input • Playing it safe	• Open • Accepting diverse points of view • Crowd-sourced • Courageous

CAUSES, CONSEQUENCES & COMPLICATIONS OF LACK OF STRATEGIC THINKING

Falling Behind

Lack of Alignment

Confused

Lack of Strategic-Thinking

Personal   Professional

Decreased Buyin

Disengaged

Decreased Quality

Less Creativity

Toxic Culture

Many executive leaders believe they need to work on being more strategic. There are many potential reasons for this. One is that strategic thinking is learned through practice. Sadly, many companies do not engage leaders early in their careers in strategic thinking and planning exercises, leaving new leaders underdeveloped. Another everyday reality is that many leaders are bombarded with decisions requiring immediate attention throughout their day. Their focus and comfort get pulled toward working on the urgent versus the important. Also, what gets measured gets rewarded.

However, many strategic priorities do not have frequent measures to reinforce leaders' focus on strategic thinking. Assumptions and biases can also cause leaders to find data points that support their point of view. These assumptions and biases provide further evidence for why leaders do not need to risk transparency and engage others in strategic thinking activities.

The complications associated with a lack of strategic thinking extend beyond the organization. In addition to the apparent lack of alignment and influence, leaders who lack strategic thinking find it harder to achieve personal and professional success and significance. When focused on winning the day, it is easy to fall behind, which can be disastrous in a highly competitive marketplace.

Also, followers who are excluded from strategic planning lack buy-in to organizational strategies. They quickly become confused about the company's direction and are disengaged. A lack of inclusivity with strategic thinking lowers quality and creativity. Also, an exclusive approach to strategic thinking can reinforce a toxic culture that values certain groups within a company over others.

TRANSFORMATIONAL TOOLS & EXERCISES FOR THINKING STRATEGICALLY

How to Increase Your Strategic Focal Length. The Futures Wheel is a simple tool that can be used to forecast indirect and direct consequences with an event, change, or trend.[7] It can be used as an entry into strategic planning or a way to evaluate an emerging trend in light of existing strategies. The tool promotes learning through collaboration with others on a brainstormed sequence or order of

LIFE-CHANGING HABIT #10: THINKING STRATEGICALLY

consequences. The following provides an overview of the steps taken by using the tool:

- The first step is to determine the trend or potential event that you need to consider. The trend of smart cities will be used in this example.
- The second step is to reflect on the social, technological, economic, environmental, political, legal, and ethical categories as they relate to your event or trend. In this example, these categories would relate to smart cities. The goal is to capture as many ideas as you can, then go back and consider the impacts. Some impacts might be positive; others might be unfavorable. Note: Don't worry about getting this perfect, just capture your ideas.
- The third step is to get rid of duplicates and group ideas that make sense before moving forward.
- The fourth step involves another round to understand what might occur next. Once again, get rid of duplicates and group ideas that make sense before moving forward.
- The final step is to repeat the prior step for the second-order consequences.

How to Plan for Mixed Realities. Scenario planning is a decision-making tool leaders can use to explore and understand a variety of possible issues impacting organizations. Since leaders cannot predict the future, both learning and preparation are critical. The goal is for leaders and followers to extend their focal length by considering what multiple futures might bring. Scenario planning involves identifying a specific set of uncertainties, i.e., different possibilities of what might happen in the future. Wind tunneling is a term sometimes used for the basic concept embedded with scenario planning that allows the organization to be tested in a variety of turbulent times. Strategic thinking requires the ability to scan the environment to identify the significant trends and weak signals of potential, such as potentially emerging issue or opportunity.

Typical approaches to scenario planning involve the following steps:

- Identify a focus question
- Identify critical environmental factors
- Identify driving forces
- Rank critical uncertainties
- Choose the main themes—most uncertain and essential forces
- Develop scenarios
- Examine implications of the scenarios, and
- Identify ways to monitor changes

Scenario planning helps organizations focus on those likely and critical external elements impacting the business and to think creatively about the situation. The benefits of scenario planning include changed thinking, consideration of possible futures, improved decision-making, and enhanced organizational learning and imagination.

How to Measure Critical Thinking Capacity. It is crucial to comprehend and analyze various situations in strategic thinking. A leader's ability to question and make connections between ideas and options improves strategic thinking. Various psychometric assessments measure a leader's critical thinking capability and improvement. The Watson Glaser Critical Thinking Appraisal is one valid measure based on a leader's ability to recognize assumptions, evaluate arguments, and draw conclusions. For more information on the Watson Glaser Critical Thinking Appraisal, visit www.talentlens.com.

How to Build Strategic Leadership Business Acumen. Leaders and teams looking to build their strategic leadership thinking, acting, and influencing business acumen can benefit from using the Strategic Team Review and Action Tool (STRAT). The STRAT measures a

LIFE-CHANGING HABIT #10: THINKING STRATEGICALLY

strategic leadership team's capability on the following twelve attributes using a self-reporting assessment:

- Assess Internal and External Environments
- Clarify Mission, Vision, and Values
- Discover and Prioritize Drivers
- Create Business Strategies
- Develop Business Strategies
- Execute, Perform, and Learn
- Lead Change
- Shape Culture
- Decision-Making
- Leverage Priorities
- Direction, Alignment, and Commitment
- Leadership Effectiveness

After completing the assessment, it is helpful to work with a facilitator to analyze and debrief the team-specific data with the norm data before deciding where to focus using root cause analysis approaches. For a copy of the survey and more information on the STRAT, read *Becoming a Strategic Leader: Your Role in Your Organization's Enduring Success* by Hughes, Beatty, and Dinwoodie.[8]

How to Conduct Strategic Workforce Planning (SWP). No organizational result is achieved without someone doing something. Now, more than ever, businesses need to proactively get the right people, in the right place, at the right time, and at the right cost to execute strategies. Skill gaps and talent shortages make it impossible for organizations to succeed. Businesses need strategic workforce plans that are dynamic enough to enable organizations to thrive today and in the future. A common approach to SWP aligns a business strategy with a workforce plan with the following three core steps:

- **Role segmentation.** Identify strategic roles based on their importance to the execution of the business strategy. As a general guide, identify the roles that will contribute the most value to the strategy. These roles would account for no more than 15 percent of the organization.
- **Environmental scanning.** Quantitative and qualitative analysis of the internal and external workforce supply and demand.
- **Scenario planning.** Consider a range of potential futures to improve the possibilities of future success. Possible future scenarios might include unionization, competitive threats, availability of talent, or economic recovery impact on the workforce. The goal is not to predict the future but to prepare for likely possibilities.

KEY POINTS—THINKING STRATEGICALLY

- Organizations desperately need leaders to adopt an approach to strategic thinking that accounts for the volatility and uncertainty in the marketplace.
- Being successful and adaptive with strategic thinking requires leaders to think creatively and practically about the future.
- It is dangerous when employees don't understand the why behind their work.
- Without a well-defined strategy, it is difficult for followers to navigate conflicts and confusion created by disruptive change and ambiguity.
- The best strategies are developed inclusive of followers, focus on helping others for a greater good, account for mixed future realities, and are implemented.
- A significant downfall of strategic thinking is that leaders often fail to consider future environmental changes.

LIFE-CHANGING HABIT #10: THINKING STRATEGICALLY

- Strategic foresight helps leaders identify signs of emerging trends in the margins, that is, not what is widely known, resulting in actions an organization takes to prepare for the future.
- Farsighted leaders can position organizations to move from responding and reacting to change to creating trends and being the first to market.
- Leveraging diversity enhances strategic thinking creativity, engagement, and strategy quality.
- Creative ideas reflective of the customer's stated and unstated needs come from those closest to the customer and with no stake in the status quo.
- Advances in technology enable a more inclusive, timely, and less costly approach to inclusive and transparent strategic thinking.
- Potential drawbacks with inclusive strategic thinking are bias, agility, and communication effectiveness.

REFLECTION QUESTIONS—THINKING STRATEGICALLY

- Do you have a clear personal and professional vision for the next three to five years?
- What are your current strategy's likely long-range strengths, weaknesses, threats, and opportunities?
- Does your current strategy account for the likely different potential futures?
- Have different segments of the organization had meaningful input into the current strategy? What is the truth in the feedback received? What are you missing?
- Do you monitor the market for long-range threats and opportunities?
- What strategic "skills gaps" need to be addressed in the short- and long-term?

- How much time each week do you spend thinking about the big picture?
- Is the organization aware of the strategy? Does the organization understand the strategy?

• • •

Endnotes

1. Bennis, W. (2008). "Leadership is the capacity to translate vision into reality." *Journal of Property Management, 73*(5), 13.
2. Hughes, R.L., Beatty, K.M., & Dinwoodie, D. (2014). *Becoming a Strategic Leader: Your Role in Your Organization's Enduring Success* (Second ed.) Jossey-Bass.
3. Kaplan, R.S., Norton, D.P. (2005). "The Office of Strategy Management." *Harvard Business Review,* 83(10):72-80
4. Nwachukwu, C., Chladkova, H., & Olatunji, F. (2018). "The Relationship between Employee Commitment to Strategy Implementation and Employee Satisfaction." *Trends Economics and Management,* 12(31), 46-56. doi:10.13164/trends.2018.31.45
5. Amrollahi, A., & Rowlands, B. (2018). "OSPM: A design methodology for open strategic planning." *Information & Management, 55*(6), 667-685. https://doi.org/10.1016/j.im.2018.01.006
6. Amrollahi, A., & Rowlands, B. (2017). "Collaborative open strategic planning: A method and case study." *Information Technology & People,* 30(4), 832-852. https://doi.org/10.1108/ITP-12-2015-0310
7. Glenn, J. (1972). "Futurizing teaching vs futures course." *Social Science Record,* 9(3).
8. Hughes, R.L., Beatty, K.M., & Dinwoodie, D. (2014). *Becoming a Strategic Leader: Your Role in Your Organization's Enduring Success* (Second ed.) Jossey-Bass.

PART THREE

Secrets to Leading with Life-Changing Habits

"We must be the change we wish to see in the world."
—GAHNDI[1]

Endnotes
1. Shapiro, F. (2021). *The New Yale Book of Quotations*. Yale University Press.

PART THREE

Secrets to Leading with Life-Changing Faith

Answering Questions and Anticipating Problems

> "The chains of habit are too weak to be felt until they are too strong to be broken."
> —SAMUEL JOHNSON[1]

The topic of life-changing leadership habits typically generates questions that are occasionally followed by a few objections. Unfortunately, breaking old habits and creating new ones is never easy. What follows is not intended to be an exhaustive list of every potential question or objection you may have or encounter. Instead, these are a few of the more common questions and biggest challenges you may confront while creating life-changing leadership habits. Hopefully, these answers eliminate some confusion you may have.

COMMON QUESTIONS

The first question I tend to get when talking about life-changing leadership habits is, what are they? The answer to this question has been addressed in Part Two of this book. The following are a few of the more common questions that tend to follow.

If bad habits have so many negative consequences, why do leaders exhibit them?
After an exhaustive review of the literature, the evidence in peer-reviewed journals suggests that leaders adopt bad leadership habits because they are bad people. (I'm just kidding.) It is impossible to answer this question definitively as the why is connected to the person and the situation. People differ in how they respond to the same situations and in the everyday habits they adopt. I have observed that leaders can surprise you—for better or worse. The larger the surprise, the harder we look for a definitive reason as to why.

What is the best way to approach breaking a bad habit?
Proven strategies to break bad habits include avoiding what drains your self-control, building your self-control, strength, and endurance, replacing a bad habit with a life-changing habit, and changing circumstances that trigger the bad habit.

Like physical strength, our capacity for self-control is limited.[2] Willpower used repeatedly creates the kind of fatigue we experience when exercising. Studies have revealed that dealing with physical stress, emotional distress, and constantly resisting bad habits drains our willpower. However, not all situations drain our capacity for self-control equally. Resisting tempting food might require more or less willpower than choosing to exercise and endure physical pain. The amount of willpower drained depends on the situation and your level of endurance and strength. If you struggle with eating too many sweets, you don't want to work remotely from a donut shop.

Like physical endurance, strength can be enhanced with training, and self-control is proven to improve with training.[3] Practicing small acts of self-control—like avoiding desirable food or exercise followed by periods of rest—builds self-control. While the specific self-control activity you practice is not essential, the amount of self-control exerted is critical. In other words, it is not what type of weight-lifting you do, but how much weight you lift. Using a coach and making the practice visible are excellent ways to start practicing self-control.

Your world is perfectly designed for you to exhibit the habits you have right now. You are getting some physical, social, or emotional benefit from your current habits. In Part Two of this book, I have provided suggested virtues or life-changing habits to replace identified leadership vices or bad habits.

When breaking bad habits, you need to pick a life-changing habit to start. It doesn't matter which habit, just that you choose one to start. For example, when I wanted to get control of my weight, I adopted a habit of weighing my portions of food. Whatever habit you want to break, you must plan what you will do to change your bad habit.

Much of our day is defined by repetition. Disrupting the daily routine helps to reduce the cues that prompt habits. Becoming aware of what triggers a bad habit is the first step to finding a way to disrupt the context of our routine. Both physical location and the presence of others can be potent disruptors to our routine's context.[4] For example, suppose you are trying to break the bad leadership habit of tolerating poor performance. In that case, you could engage your leader in looking over performance reviews before finalizing them.

What is the best way to create a life-changing leadership habit?
Start with a development plan. You may have heard the saying that if you fail to plan, you plan to fail. There is no one-size-fits-all template. However, your plan, at a minimum, should include your why, the belief that you can change, how to make that change easy and automatic, as well as planning for accountability and for falling forward.

Starting with why you want and need to make a change and believing you can change are significant first steps. Clarifying your specific why helps associate value with the new habit and increases the likelihood the change will occur. To find your why, reflect on how the new habit will benefit your success and significance, as well as its impact on significant others and your community.

For example, you may not be as motivated to improve your health for your benefit. However, when you think about your family, the value of implementing new life-changing habits may be more significant. In planning for your new habit, you want to visualize succeeding. There is a reason you see athletes before a competition practicing for the game. See yourself building life-changing habits and achieving success and significance.

Don't try to make too many changes at once. Make it easy. When creating a new habit, pick one change to make that's easy, then gradually increase the number of changes you wish to make. Multiple changes at once make creating a new habit more difficult. Suppose your goal is to lead with the life-changing habit of appreciative thinking. Rather than starting with implementing an appreciative inquiry summit or redesigning your organization's approach to strategic planning, pick one appreciative question to incorporate into existing one-to-one meetings. Keeping it simple to start allows you to build on success.

Habit stacking is a proven approach for getting a new habit started and making it automatic. Habit stacking involves connecting new habits with existing habits to make them memorable. Suppose you are looking to create a habit of saying *thank you* to your team. In that case, you could benefit from connecting this with another behavior you have already formed. For example, if you walk through your facility each day to check on production status, you could start using that time to catch your team doing something valuable and immediately say thank you. Pairing new habits with existing routines is proven to make the new habit more memorable and establishes automaticity.

Life is not meant to be lived alone. Too often, we fail to consider how we can leverage accountability to help us create a life-changing habit. Being accountable to ourselves and someone we trust is proven to help create a new habit.[5] Conducting check-in meetings with your accountability partner will increase motivation and habit consistency. We all tend to do better when someone is watching, even if that someone is you. Daily reflection combined with considering opportunities to improve establishes personal accountability and creates a continuous improvement mindset.

Plan for falling forward—not backward. When you first learned to walk, you fell more than you walked. You are human, and failure comes only when we give up. Being consistent, not perfect, is essential for creating a new habit. Develop a plan for how you will get back on track when you fall. It's not that you are expecting to fail, but think ahead for how you will get back up. Creating new habits is not a game of all or nothing.

How helpful is reading a book to break bad leadership habits?
You may be surprised. Knowing is the same as doing, and at the end of the day, you need both. When you are unaware that you have a bad habit, a book based on proven research creates awareness leading to transformational thinking and actions. Books help generate awareness and motivate you to take action. However, when you already know you have a bad habit and know what to do, reading a book is probably not your best course of action.

No one in my organization is helping me lead with life-changing habits. What should I do?
The need for workplace development has never been more urgent. The pressures of a crisis-driven workplace disrupt routines and habits. Leaders are facing many new challenges. If you are not continuously developing, you are falling behind. Unfortunately, the higher up you move in an organization, the less coaching you often receive from within the company. The solution is to hire an executive coach. An extensive quantitative study revealed that executives receiving coaching increased goal achievement

significantly (over 82 percent) compared with experienced executives receiving no coaching.[6] Also, some of the most admired companies in the Fortune 100 contribute to the fast-growing executive coaching industry. Broad support for executive coaching and its effectiveness is undeniable.

What do you do if the company culture is reinforcing a leadership bad habit?
Organizational culture is the one thing that influences everything in a company. The closer your association to the organization, the greater the culture's pull has on your habits.[7] A sense of belonging and peer pressure are powerful influencers. Also, not all habits are equally difficult to break. One of your best strategies, when faced with this dilemma, is to modify your situation. You can choose to try and change the company culture or join a new team or company where the culture better aligns with your desired habits. You can also choose to do nothing and be miserable. But this is not recommended, and you are unlikely to achieve success and significance.

COMMON PROBLEMS FROM LEADERS

Typically, leaders want to become better leaders. That is likely why you are reading this book. However, even in the process of making positive life changes, we can encounter problems. The following are a few of the more common objections you may have and some thoughts on overcoming these problems.

I do not have the time to change my leadership habits.
One of the most common legitimate objections I hear is that "I don't have time for this." In most cases, building life-changing habits and breaking bad ones does not happen overnight. It takes time, practice, and consistency. We all get the same amount of time in a day. As business owners and executives, finding time to invest in your development

is challenging and often comes with feelings of guilt from the trade-offs you must make. However, how you choose to spend your time is visible to others and sends a message to the rest of your company.

If you invest time developing yourself, you will reinforce a learning culture where individual development is valued. Additionally, it is essential to remember that your bad habits are costing you in ways that impact people, profit, and purpose.

I have real work to get done.
This is similar to the objection of having limited time but with the twist that an either-or decision must be made. For example: "I have only so many hours in the day, and I can either get the work done that our customers need or spend time developing myself." This argument takes a nearsighted view on value. It minimizes the costs of bad habits on the leader, their team, their business success, and their significance. It is like a belief that taking the time to sharpen a saw is too costly when compared to the value of continuing to cut wood with a dull saw. Creating life-changing habits increases the leader's capacity and effectiveness—with long-term returns on the initial investment of time.

These bad habits were good habits in the past. These life-changing habits will soon become bad habits as well.
A topic like leadership means different things to different people. The many competing points of view on what makes for good leadership create confusion. What's more, the unregulated leadership development industry has more than a few ideas based on smoke and mirrors to sell ideas rather than research. Additionally, the same approach can have different results in different situations and with different people. For example, suppose I am about to make a life-threatening mistake. In that case, I appreciate direct and forceful communication to help me stop. However, when the stakes are not that high, I interpret that same behavior as obnoxious.

I have tried to break bad habits in the past and failed.
Most of us have tried to break a habit before, only to keep doing what we don't want to do. Although not the most common objection I hear, this is a shared experience. When you view the process of breaking habits with a pass-fail mental model, it sets you up for frustration. Breaking strong bad habits is a learning process. You must realize that the only failure is giving up. If you are struggling with this objection, it is helpful to answer why you are trying to break this habit in the first place.

My situation is different; these life-changing habits won't work for me.
It is essential to know your habits and routines. However, leadership is not something we are born with, and we are much more alike than we may appear. I say that because I find leaders from all walks of life, in all sizes of companies, across diverse industries, who believe they are the only ones struggling with a habit. These challenges are shared, and the life-changing habits in this book are proven to work.

• • •

Endnotes
1. Peter, L. (1977). *Peter's Quotations: Ideas for Our Time.* William Morrow & Co. p. 147
2. Muraven, M., Baumeister, R., & Tice, D. (1999). "Longitudinal Improvement of Self-Regulation Through Practice: Building Self-Control Strength Through Repeated Exercise." *The Journal of Social Psychology*, 139(4), 446-457. https://doi.org/10.1080/00224549909598404
3. Muraven, M., & Baumeister, R. (2000). "Self-regulation and depletion of limited resources: Does self-control resemble a muscle?" *Psychological Bulletin*, 126(2), 247-259. https://doi.org/10.1037/0033-2909.126.2.247
4. Wood, W., Tam, L., & Witt, M. G. (2005). "Changing circumstances, disrupting habits." *Journal of Personality and Social Psychology*, 88(6), 918-933. https://doi.org/10.1037/0022-3514.88.6.918
5. Cleo, G., Glasziou, P., Beller, E., Isenring, E., & Rae, T. (2019). "Habit-based interventions for weight loss maintenance in adults with overweight and obesity: a randomized controlled trial." *International Journal of Obesity*, 43(2), 374-383. http://dx.doi.org/10.1038/s41366-018-0067-4

6. Bowles, Cunningham, C. J. L., De La Rosa, G. M., & Picano, J. (2007). "Coaching leaders in middle and executive management: goals, performance, buy-in." *Leadership & Organization Development Journal, 28*(5), 388–408. https://doi.org/10.1108/01437730710761715
7. Clear, J. (2018). *Atomic Habits: Tiny Changes, Remarkable Results: An Easy & Proven Way to Build Good Habits & Break Bad Ones.* Avery.

Are There Any Downsides to Building Life-Changing Habits?

Building life-changing habits take time.
A common myth is that it takes twenty-one days to build a habit. The number of times you must perform a life-changing habit before it becomes routine can vary substantially from person to person and situation to situation. One study concluded it typically ranges from 18 to 254 days of consistency.[1] The key is repetition, and eventually, a new habit will emerge.

Bad habits are often enjoyable and automatic.
I don't consider myself a bad person, yet I struggle with the life-changing habit of living in balance. I know eating more food than a typical serving has adverse health consequences. However, I still struggle not to treat myself and overindulge.

Often, our brain works against us by reinforcing bad habits. Some bad habits produce pleasure that triggers the release of the brain chemical dopamine as a reward. Dopamine is a neurotransmitter that helps us focus and regulates many different parts of brain function including heart rate, motivation, mood, learning, and pleasure. It influences feelings that reinforce habits. We are wired for repetition and doing things automatically. This creates advantages for performing a task without concentrating, yet it also makes it harder to change habits.

Good intentions are not enough to break bad habits. However, leaders are not doomed to live with bad leadership habits; you can change and reorient your behavior. Self-control is the ability to act appropriately despite the difficulty. A crisis-driven workplace drains self-control. When we run out of self-control, we are less likely to resist leadership bad habits. The good news is that self-control is something leaders can build, making it easier to stand firm and be the leader the world needs them to be.

Building life-changing habits create the feeling of being stuck.
As you work on building new habits, it is not uncommon to feel stuck. Whether you've just started your journey or have been working on your habit for months, it doesn't matter. Anyone who has tried to build a new habit or break a bad one has encountered the feeling of being stuck.

Occasionally, you're not really stuck, but changes are not noticeable or not happening at the pace you desire. Small changes can be difficult to notice when comparing changes day-to-day. Also, improvement doesn't always happen in a linear or exponential way you desire. It is good to keep in mind that slowing down or changing your expectations might be the best course of action.

It's also possible that there's some part of a bad habit you don't want to give up. Sometimes, you can sabotage your progress by avoiding working on breaking your bad habit. If you feel stuck, a good strategy is to talk with a trusted advisor who can listen, provide perspective, and hold you accountable to take action.

An executive coach can be an excellent trusted advisor who provides a goal-oriented, solution-focused process in which you collaboratively build action plans and take steps toward your goal.

• • •

ARE THERE ANY DOWNSIDES TO BUILDING LIFE-CHANGING HABITS?

Endnotes
1. Lally, P., van Jaarsveld, Cornelia H., Potts, H., & Wardle, J. (2010). "How are habits formed: Modelling habit formation in the real world." *European Journal of Social Psychology*, 40(6), 998-1009. https://doi.org/10.1002/ejsp.674

Concluding Thoughts

I learned an important life lesson on a business trip to Puerto Rico while traveling with a good friend. We tried to travel together for work whenever possible because it made traveling more fun. My friend was a self-proclaimed "propeller-head" and always had the latest technology. I counted on him for directions because he always brought his GPS. (This was before the invention of the smartphone.) At the time, few people had a GPS for routine navigation. After picking up our rental car at the airport, we realized he hadn't programmed the GPS with the address of our hotel. His GPS could tell us where we were in the world within about ten feet. But without knowing where we were going, it was useless information.

This experience taught me that it doesn't matter if you know where you are. What matters most in life is if you know where you are going. The secret to creating life-changing leadership habits is not only having a greater self-awareness, but in better defining—or redefining—effective leadership. You will not achieve the best of what can be without a clear picture.

Over the course of this guide, we have looked at the influence of our inner and outer games on leadership. We have explored the vices, virtues, and complications associated with breaking ten leadership bad habits. And we've discussed transformational ideas grounded in the latest research that you can immediately integrate into your leadership habits.

Bad habits come with costly consequences that impact more than just the leader. They extend to those we lead, our businesses, and our communities. You can design a better future when you live and lead with purpose. Striving for life-changing leadership habits is a competitive advantage available to any leader looking for a powerful point of differentiation. Breaking bad habits is possible but not easy. Like hiking, the first step begins by being entirely willing to take a step and make a change.

As this book draws to a close, I hope you achieve your goals and are the leader the contemporary world needs. We are all more connected than we perceive. Never stop growing personally and professionally. Your success and significance do not have a finish line. They arise in the pursuit of your dreams.

• • •

Appendix

Appendix

What Should You Read Next?

Thank you for taking the time to read this book. Nothing is more satisfying than helping leaders elevate people, profit, and purpose. It has been a great pleasure to share my experiences and these proven practices with you. If you are looking for something to read next, I have a suggestion.

If you enjoyed *Life-Changing Leadership Habits*, then you may like my other writing as well. Sign up at www.organizationalespresso.com to get my latest articles sent directly to your inbox in my free weekly newsletter.

Subscribers are also the first to hear about my new projects and future books. In addition to my own work, I send out a reading list of my favorite books from other authors with ideas that will stimulate individual, team, and organizational effectiveness.

Please sign up today at: www.organizationalespresso.com

• • •

Bonus Resources

Do you have a friend or work for a leader who needs to learn how to lead with life-changing habits and break one of the ten leadership worst habits? You are not alone. The leadership bad habits discussed are commonly encountered whether you are working for a fast-paced, growing start-up or a Fortune 500 company with well-defined processes and systems. When I speak with leaders about this book, I'm frequently asked how they can help others. So I've compiled the following practical and proven advice into what I hope you will find useful as you help others be the leaders the world needs.

Download this bonus guide, "What Are the Best Ways to Help Others Lead with Life-Changing Habits?" and claim additional free bonus resources at www.lifechangingleadershiphabits.com

• • •

Acknowledgments

I have relied heavily on my relationship with God and my professional network during the creation of this book. Before anyone else, I must thank my wife, Kelly, who has been instrumental throughout this process. She played every role possible in partnering with me on this book: spouse, friend, fan, critic, editor, and therapist. It is no exaggeration that I could not have created this book without her. As in our entire married life, we have done this together.

Second, I am grateful to my family, not just for their encouragement but for loving me no matter what journey I take in life. I have benefited from many different perspectives and years of wisdom from my children, parents, and relatives. In particular, I want my mom and dad to know that I have genuinely cherished their daily prayers and having them as my biggest fans. I have benefited from knowing that my children, Cole, Morgan, and Mackenzie, love me unconditionally and see only the best in their dad. Also, having Aunt Meg, Uncle Glenn, and Uncle Howard share their years of writing and book publishing experience has been a true gift.

Third, I want to thank my final project chair, Dr. Diane Wiater, my rough-draft reviewer, Jeri Vettel, and my doctoral cohort peer, Jay Hawthorne. Their talents and skills have been indispensable to my critical thinking for this book. I am deeply grateful for their prayers, friendship, and wisdom.

As for the content, I have a long list of people to thank. To start, there are a few people from whom I have learned so much that I need to mention them by name. Dr. Kevin Munson, Dr. Darryl Wahlstrom, Dr. Keith Ruckstuhl, Bob Donovan, David Beach, and Shawn Ishler have been friends, and each influenced my thoughts on leadership habits in different and meaningful ways throughout my career. I thank Dr. Kathleen Patterson, Dr. Gary Oster (†), Dr. Debra Dean, Dr. William Winner, Dr. Bruce Winston, Dr. Arthur Satterwhite III, Dr. Rob Freeborough, and Dr. Russell Huizing for their guidance during my doctoral studies in strategic leadership.

In deciding the topics to include in this book and reading early versions of it, I have benefited from the guidance of my professional network. Thanks to Andy Corbus, Barbi Brewer-Watson, Chris Shride, Dan Duba, Dick DeWitt, Dr. Edna Marangu, Dr. Gia Suggs, Dr. Kelly Whelan, Greg Boisture, Hayward Suggs, Jeff Veeser, Dr. Jeremy VanKley, Jill Day, Kristine Babcock, Laurel Romanella, Mary Verstraete, Matt Henry, Dr. Ralph Mortenson, Dr. Ryan Spittal, Dr. Steve Griffin, Tim Nelson, Tom Ascher, Tom Murray, Dr. Toni Pauls, and Walter Rogers.

Writing a book is like driving a car at night in a snowstorm. You can only see as far as the headlights shine, and you can feel lost at times. To the many friends and extended family members who asked, "How is the book going?" and offered a word of encouragement when needed but not requested—thank you!

• • •

Accidental Habit Assessment

> "The unexamined life is not worth living."
> —SOCRATES[1]

Few leaders seek to develop bad habits. Everyone I know strives for good habits. That is why this quiz is labeled the Accidental Habit Assessment (A.H.A.). It helps you uncover possible leadership bad habits that are keeping you from getting the most out of life and work. It will take you five to ten minutes to complete the quiz. In addition to discovering your "Aha," the quiz provides you with a personalized reading guide to help you get the most value out of this book in the least amount of time.

You can take this quiz at www.lifechangingleadershiphabits.com

• • •

Endnotes
1. Brickhouse, Thomas C.; Smith, Nicholas D. (1994). *Plato's Socrates*. Oxford University Press.

Index

#
360 evaluation, 92

A
A.H.A. (Accidental Habit Assessment), 253
ABC model (antecedents, behavior, consequences), performance and, 40
absence of humility, 44–45
absence of love for followers, 43, 47–48
active listening, 136
　empathic, 137
　encouraging in others, 150
　nonverbal, 137
　skill development, 150–151
　verbal, 137
addiction *versus* habit, 32
affinity groups, 118
AI (Appreciative Inquiry), 58
architecting culture, 198
argumentativeness scale, conversation management, 171–173
artifacts, culture and, 18

atychiphobia, 204
audience effects, social facilitation, 13–15

B
basic assumptions, culture and, 18
behavior, ABC model, 40
Behavior Engineering Model, 50
body language, active listening, 137
burnout, ProQOL and, 128

C
change, 31–32
character, 7–8
CliftonStrengths Assessment, 67–68
co-action effects, social facilitation, 13–15
coaching, learning mindset and, 198
coercive leadership, 145–146
common problems, 234–236
common questions, 229–234
communication
　emotion micromanagement, 171
　micromanaging flow, 170

strategic thinking and, 215
community, living in balance and, 117
   affinity groups, 118
   CoP (communities of practice), 117
   peer advisory groups, 117
compassion, 36
conflict mismanagement, 166
conflict skills development, 169–170
consequences, ABC model, 40–41
conversations, difficult, mismanaging, 28
CoP (communities of practice), 117
credibility, 24
   transparency and, 180–181
culture, 17–18

D

data-driven decision-making, lack, 28
data-driven decisions, embracing, 71
   analytic organization design, 84–85
   assessing culture, 82–83
   case study, 77–78
   data-driven cultural orientation, 73–75
   data-driven decision making, 72
   Descriptive Data Analytics, 72
   lack, 78–80
   organization design, 75–77
   Predictive Data Analytics, 72
   reflection questions, 86
   virtues, 73–77
delegation, 95–96
   ineffective, 99–102
diagnostic evaluation, 92
discretionary effort, 24
   performance, 41

downsides to building life-changing habits, 239–240

E

empathic active listening, 137
empathy, 36
employee retention, 24
empowering followers, 140–141
exclusive strategic thinking, 218–220
executing what is important, 93–95
explicit reliability, 182

F

failure
   atychiphobia, 204
   embracing, defining, 196
   fear of, 29
      overcoming, 206
   fear of failure, 29
      collaboration and, 206–207
      game theory and, 206
      mindfulness and, 206
   game theory and, 206
   lack of success, 196
   measuring fear of, 205–206
   mindfulness and, 206
   supporting, 198–199
failure, embracing
   case study, 199–201
   defining, 196
   fear of failure, 202–207
   learning mindset and, 197–198
   reflection questions, 209
   supporting failure, 198–199
   virtues, 197–199
FFM (Five-Factor Model), 11–12
followers
   disempowering, 146–147
   empowering, 140–141
   love for, 27, 35

INDEX

absence, 47
humility, 39
performance reinforcement, 39–41
reflection questions, 51–52
servant leadership style and, 37–38
transactional leadership style, 41–48

G
game theory, fear of failure and, 206

H
habits. *See also* life-changing habits
  versus addiction, 32
  bad
    breaking, 230–231
    company culture and, 234
  inner game and, 5
humility, 39
  absence (*See* narcissism)
  examples, 45
  measuring, 49

I
ICF (International Coaching Federation), 190
implicit reliability, 182
inclusive strategic thinking, 215
influence, creating, 138–140
inner game, 5
innovation, 24
intrinsic motivation, 141
isolating behavior, living in balance and, 123–124

J-K
job expectations management, 115
knowing yourself, 91–93

L
leadership
  benefits, 23–25
  as conversation, 25
  preferred approach, 151
  unintentional, 28
leadership crisis, World Economic Form on, 3
leadership styles
  servant, 37–38
  transactional, 41–48
learning mindset, 197–198
life-changing habits
  being trustworthy, 179–180
    absence of, 185–189
    case study, 184–185
    reflection questions, 192–193
    relationship trust assessment, 189–190
    relationships, 180
    transparency, 180
    trustworthiness definition, 180
    virtues, 180–183
    work style and, 190–191
  downsides to building, 239–240
  embracing data-driven decisions, 71
    analytic organization design, 84–85
    assessing culture, 82–83
    case study, 77–78
    data-driven cultural orientation, 73–75
    data-driven decision making, 72
    Descriptive Data Analytics, 72
    lack, 78–82
    organization design, 75–77
    Predictive Data Analytics, 72
    reflection questions, 86
    virtues, 73–77

embracing failure, 195
  case study, 199–201
  fear of failure
    collaboration and, 206–207
    examples, 201–205
    measuring, 205–206
    overcoming, 206
  reflection questions, 209
  virtues, 197–199
excelling in management,
    135–136
  active listening and, 136–138,
    150–151
  case study, 142–144
  coercion, 145–146
  creating influence and,
    138–140
  disempowering followers,
    146–147
  empowering followers, 140–141
  leadership approaches, 151
  macromanagement, 144–149
  micromanagement, 144–149
  mismatched management,
    147–149
  partnering, 141–142
  reflection questions, 152–153
  selective listening, 144–145
  virtues, 136–142
focusing on strengths, 55–56
  appreciative framing, 66
  appreciative interviews, 66–67
  case study, 59–61
  CliftonStrengths Assessment,
    67–68
  failure to see what might be,
    61–65
  identifying strengths, 67–68
  reflection questions, 68
  reward and recognition, 56–57

reward and recognition
  improvements, 65–66
  strengths thinking, 57–59
  strengths-focus definition, 56
  VIA Character Strengths
    Survey, 67
  virtues, 56–59
living in balance, 113–114
  boundary management,
    128–130
  burnout, measuring, 128
  case study, 119–120
  defining, 114
  network, increasing, 130–132
  reflective questions, 132–133
  saying no, 127
  self-care, practicing, 130
  unbalanced living examples,
    120–127
  virtues, 114–119
loving followers, 35
  absence, examples, 43–48
  Behavior Engineering Model,
    50
  humility, 39, 49
  performance consequences, 49
  performance controls, 50
  performance reinforcement,
    39–41
  reflection questions, 51–52
  selfless love, 36–37
  servant leadership evaluation,
    48–49
  servant leadership style, 37–38
  transactional leadership style,
    41–48
mastering difficult conversations,
    155–156
  case study, 163–164
  competence, 171–173

INDEX

conflict skills development, 169–170
control traps, avoiding, 170–171
levels of conversations, 162–163
mismanagement examples, 165–169
productive conflict, 159–162
reflection questions, 176
upward dissent, 173–175
vulnerability and, 156–159
maximizing purpose, 89
360-Degree assessments, 102–103
case study, 96–97
purpose, discovering, 104
purpose definition, 90–91
reflection questions, 109
self-regulation improvements, 103–104
team meeting effectiveness, 105–106
unintentional leadership, 97–102
urgent *vs.* important, 104–105
virtual meeting effectiveness, 106–108
virtues, 91–96
thinking strategically, 211
case study, 215–217
common sense and, 212
critical thinking and, 222
definition, 212–213
lack of, examples, 217–220
mixed realities and, 221–222
reflection questions, 225–226
reframing and, 212
scanning and, 212
STRAT (Strategic Team Review and Action Tool), 222–223

strategic focal length, 220–221
strategic leadership business acumen, 222–223
SWP (Strategic Workforce Planning), 223–224
systems thinking, 213
virtues, 213–215
visioning and, 212
listening
active listening, 136–137, 150
selective listening, 144–145
living in balance, 113–114
boundary management, 128–130
burnout, measuring, 128
case study, 119–120
community and, 117–118
defining, 114
isolating behavior, 123–124
job expectations management, 115
mismanagement, 120–121
network, increasing, 130–132
reflective questions, 132–133
saying no, 127
self-care, 115–117
practicing, 130
self-sabotage, 121–123
unbalanced living examples, 120–127
virtues, 114–119
work-life boundary management, 118–119
mismanagement, 124–126
love, selfless, 35–36
loving followers, 27, 35
absence, examples, 43–48
Behavior Engineering Model, 50
humility, 39, 49
performance
consequences, 49
controls, 50

259

reinforcement, 39–41
reflection questions, 51–52
selfless love, 36–37
servant leadership evaluation, 48–49
servant leadership style, 37–38
transactional leadership style, 41–48

M

macromanagement, 28, 144–149
management, excelling in, 135–136
   active listening and, 136–138, 150–151
   case study, 142–144
   coercion, 145–146
   creating influence and, 138–140
   disempowering followers, 146–147
   empowering followers, 140–141
   leadership approaches, 151
   macromanagement, 144–149
   micromanagement, 144–149
   mismatched management, 147–149
   partnering, 141–142
   reflection questions, 152–153
   selective listening, 144–145
   virtues, 136–142
mastering difficult conversations, 155–156
   argumentativeness scale, 171–173
   case study, 163–164
   competence, 171–173
   conflict skills development, 169–170
   control traps, avoiding, 170–171
   levels of conversations, 162–163
   mismanagement
      conflict mismanagement, 166
   guardedness, 165
   productive conflict, 159–162
   reflection questions, 176
   upward dissent, 173–175
   vulnerability and feedback, 158–159
   selfless love and, 159
   transparency, 158
   what matters most, 167
maximizing purpose, 89
   360-Degree assessments, 102–103
   case study, 96–97
   delegation and, 95–96
      ineffective, 99–102
   executing what is important, 93–95
   goals, 90
   knowing yourself, 91–93
   purpose, discovering, 104
   purpose definition, 90–91
   reflection questions, 109
   self-regulation improvements, 103–104
   team meeting effectiveness, 105–106
   time management matrix, 105
   unintentional leadership, 97–102
   urgent *vs.* important, 94, 104–105
   virtual meeting effectiveness, 106–108
   virtues, 91–96
meetings
   review meetings, 106
   scrum meetings, 105
   strategic meetings, 106
   tactical meetings, 105
micromanagement, 28, 144–149
   communication flow, 170
   emotions, 171
mindset, 197–198

INDEX

mismatched management, 147–149
moral relativism, 21–22
MVP (motivation, vision, paradigm), difficult conversations and, 157

N
narcissism, 44–45
network, increasing, 130–131
nonverbal active listening, 137

O
OCB (organizational citizenship behavior), 24
   performance reinforcement, 41
   server leadership style and, 38
organizational culture, 17–19
outer game, 5

P
partnering with followers, 141–142
peer advisory groups, 117
performance
   ABC model (antecedents, behavior, consequences), 40
   consequences, 49
   controls, measuring, 50
   discretionary effort, 41
   poor, tolerating, 45–46
   reinforcing, 39–41, 46
ProQOL, burnout measure and, 128

Q
questions for startup, 31–32

R
recognition, strengths-focus, 56–57
reinforcing performance, 39–41
resources, 247, 249

review meetings, 106
reward, strengths-focus, 56–57

S
saying no, 127
scrum meetings, 105
self-care, life balance and, 115–117, 130
self-sabotage, living in balance and, 121–123
selfless love, 35–36
   absence, 47–48
   definition, 36–37
   vulnerability in difficult conversations, 159
servant leadership style, 37–38
   evaluating, 48
      humility, 49
      performance consequences, 49
      performance controls, 50
   examples, 44
   humility and, 39
   transactional leadership style comparison, 44
social facilitation, 13–15
spoken values, culture and, 18
STRAT (Strategic Team Review and Action Tool), 222–223
strategic meetings, 106
strategic thinking, 211
   case study, 215–217
   common sense and, 212
   critical thinking and, 222
   definition, 212–213
   farsightedness and, 213–214
   inclusive, 214–215
   lack, 29, 217–220
   mixed realities and, 221–222
   reflection questions, 225–226
   reframing and, 212

scanning and, 212
STRAT (Strategic Team Review and Action Tool), 222–223
strategic focal length, 220–221
strategic leadership business acumen, 222–223
SWP (Strategic Workforce Planning), 223–224
systems thinking, 213
virtues, 213–215
visioning and, 212
strengths-focus, 55–56
appreciative framing, 66
appreciative interviews, 66–67
case study, 59–71
CliftonStrengths Assessment, 67–68
failure to see what might be, 61–65
deficit thinking and, 62–63
negative reinforcement and, 61–62, 64–65
identifying strengths, 67–68
recognition, 56–57
reflection questions, 68
reward, 56–57
reward and recognition, 56–57
reward and recognition improvements, 65–66
strengths thinking, 57–59
strengths-focus definition, 56
VIA Character Strengths Sturvey, 67
virtues, 56–59
SWP (Strategic Workforce Planning), 223–224

T
tactical meetings, 105
technology, worldview and, 22

thinking strategically. *See* strategic thinking
time management matrix, 105
TKI (Thomas-Kilmann Conflict Mode Instrument), 169–170
traits, 11–12
transactional leadership style, 41–48
trust
  absence, 28–29
  effectiveness and, 4
trustworthiness, 179–180
  absence of, 188–189
    credibility lack, 185–186
    reliability lack, 186–187
    transparency lack, 187
  case study, 184–185
  credibility and, 180–181
  definition, 180
  ICF (International Coaching Federation), 190
  reflection questions, 192–193
  relationship trust assessment, 189–190
  relationships, 180
  reliability
    explicit, 182
    implicit, 182
    transparency, 183
  transparency, 180
    increasing, 191
  virtues, 180–183
  work style and, 190–191

U
unbalanced living, 28
unintentional leadership, 28
  self-awareness, lack, 97–98

V
values, 7–8

verbal active listening, 137
VIA Institute on Character, 49
virtues, 7–8
vision, failure to consider, 27
vulnerability, 156–157
   MVP (motivation, vision, paradigm), 157

W–Z
work-life boundary management, balance and, 118–119
   styles, 128–130
World Economic Forum, on global leadership crisis, 3
worldview, 21–22
worthy performance, 39–41. *See also* performance

About the Author

"Autobiography is only to be trusted when it reveals something disgraceful. A man who gives a good account of himself is probably lying, since any life when viewed from the inside is simply a series of defeats."
—GEORGE ORWELL

Dr. Jeff Doolittle has helped business owners and executive leaders of small businesses all the way to global *Fortune 50* companies. His work is being taught in university classrooms. He is the founder of Organizational Talent Consulting, a premier executive coaching and business consulting firm for leaders and organizations interested in achieving success and significance.

Recently, he served as the associate dean of online graduate business programs for his alma mater, Olivet Nazarene University. Jeff received a Doctorate in Strategic Leadership from Regent University and is a certified International Coaching Federation executive coach.

He started and volunteers with a local ministry in his community that has helped hundreds of people on the road to recovery from life's hurts, habits, and hang-ups. He considers himself an organizational naturalist and *pracademic*—someone who studies organizations and is a practitioner of the latest academic research in leadership.

You can learn more about Jeff and his proven solutions by visiting his company website, organizationaltalent.com.

• • •

Organizational Talent Consulting Solutions

Coaching: Accelerate your career, shift your mindset, and live life to the fullest.

Consulting: The marketplace is turbulent and unpredictable. Together we can turn your aspirations into an advantage to achieve the greatest positive impact on your goals.

Development: Keynote presentations and leadership workshops that grow better leaders and build strong teams.

For more information on Organizational Talent Consulting, please visit organizationaltalent.com

ORGANIZATIONAL TALENT CONSULTING

I hope you enjoyed this book. Would you do me a favor?

Like all authors, I rely on online reviews to encourage future sales. Your opinion is invaluable. Would you take a few moments now to share your assessment of my book at the review site of your choice? Your opinion will help the book marketplace become more transparent and useful to all.
    Thank you very much!